ADOPTED

TWICE

MARY HANEY UNDERWOOD

ISBN: 979-8-9993216-0-2

DEDICATION

To my birth mother, Hazel. Thank you for choosing life!

To my parents, George and Grace Haney. Thank you for loving me as your own and for gifting me the legacy of God's covenant blessing and spiritual foundation.

To my husband, John. Thank you for your acceptance and unconditional love from the beginning.

To my children, Lynnette and Andrew, Michael and Laura, and Kayla. What a joy to be your mama and to see you sharing the goodness of God to the next generation. His promise to me is fulfilled through you!

To my grandchildren, Caroline, Alexandra, and Jack. My prayer is that someday you will read my story and be in awe of what the Lord did for your Grandmary. My prayer is that early on you will realize that he has done the same thing for you. Never forget that you are adopted too and that makes you children of the King.

ENDORSEMENTS FROM THE ADOPTION COMMUNITY

Adopted Twice is an honest and beautiful story of adoption that offers insights on both earthly adoption and spiritual adoption through Jesus Christ. As an adoptive mom, I have read many books about adoptions, adoptees, and adoption-related trauma. Many of those books focused on so much negativity. However, *Adopted Twice* is filled with so much hope. It is an honest account of the hard parts of adoption—loss, grief, feelings of abandonment—but also shows how God heals and redeems us through his gracious adoption of each of us.

Mary offers great perspective on the struggles that most adoptees face and that is so helpful for me as an adoptive parent. I would recommend this to any adult adoptee, adoptive parent, or anyone looking for perspective on earthly or spiritual adoption.

—**Amanda Brown**, adoptive mother and Foster the Family advocate

As a birth mother, Mary's book gave me insights into my relationship with my daughter. Sometimes, there was a wall that I couldn't breach. *Adopted Twice* helped me understand that wall and some questions I could ask to start breaking it down. *Adopted Twice* is a helpful tool for both adoptive parents and birth parents involved in open adoption. It provides much-needed hope.

—**Rose B.**, birth mother

As an adoptee and birth mother, I read Mary's book with great interest. I have read many adoptee accounts, although very few from a specifically Christian perspective. While each is unique, there are common themes often poorly understood by the broader world, including adoptees themselves. Mary's book puts flesh on these bones in a refreshing, transparent, and insightful way.

Mary invites us along on her journey, from childhood struggles to the search for and reunion with her birth mother and the ensuing years of personal and spiritual growth. She traces well the lines between the reality of her adopted state and her lived experience. She has "done the work," and it shows.

There is much here to encourage the adoptee and to enlighten those seeking to understand the adoptee experience. Too many either make being an adoptee so central as to rule their lives in a damaging way or staunchly refuse to admit to its profound effects for good or ill. Mary has grappled with both possibilities and come out with a helpful, well-integrated perspective.

—**Susan Ferrell**, adoptee and birth mother

Mary has done a beautiful job in telling her story in a brave and honest manner. She shares her pain with transparency but also shows the healing that came through therapy and other mental health services in addition to her faith journey.

My husband and I have two adopted children who grew up knowing they were adopted, knowing that was special, and understanding that it was God's plan for us to be their parents. They had enough information to satisfy their curiosity. Although they both had questions and mild struggles, they have always been confident in us as their parents and in belonging to our family.

As a birth mother who surrendered a child at 19, I definitely suffered pain and loss. I grieved quite intensely for the first year of her life. But I also trusted in God's plan for her and believed that she would have a better life with mature parents who were prepared to give her everything she needed. My birth daughter searched for and found me fifty years later. She is a lovely, well-adjusted person who grew up knowing she was adopted. She has nothing but gratitude for the choice I made.

Anyone touched by adoption experiences loss. But *Adopted Twice* provides hope that it does not have to lead to long-term adjustment problems.

—**Gail Hall**, birth mother and adoptive parent

As an adoptive parent, I have read all the most popular books on adoption wounding and trauma to give me greater insight into my child's heart and mind. *Adopted Twice* invited me into a place that none of the books have previously taken me. Through Mary's detailed account of her life journey, I got my best understanding yet of the struggles of a child placed for adoption. This book spans a vast range of emotions and lays out the tension uniquely inherent in adoption.

Mary is vulnerable about the pain and struggles she has faced despite the love, provision, and exposure to faith in Jesus she was given. She outlines with clarity the lies that fester within most adoptees and unabashedly claims the only antidote to those lies: scriptural truth and an identity in Jesus Christ. A second adoption guarantees us of an eternity without pain and brokenness.

With an air of gratitude and desperation for all to receive what she has, Mary makes it clear that *only* the choice to walk with Jesus will prepare an adoptee for an inevitable life of emotional and psychological challenges. This is a reminder for all of us, not just adoptees. What a gift to be adopted by God and what a gift this book is to adoptees and their families!

—**Denise Oorbeek**, adoptive mother and adoptee advocate

ADOPTED TWICE

MARY HANEY UNDERWOOD

TABLE OF CONTENTS

INTRODUCTION

All the days ordained for me were written in
your book before one of them came to be.
                                    —Psalm 139:16 NIV

I believe everyone has a story worth telling. I know my story needs to be shared. Not because of any great thing I have done—in fact, the opposite is true—but because my story of adoption is a story of redemption and hope. God wrote my story. Through it, he showed his faithfulness to me through not just one but two adoptions.

"Part 1: The Legacy of a Spiritual Foundation" provides the overview of my story. It tells how God knit our family together and how my parents were faithful to train us in the fear and knowledge of God. It shows how three lies became ingrained in my mind. These lies were the catalyst for what I believed to be true about myself in my teen and young adult years.

"Part 2: How Scripture Answers the Seven Core Issues in Adoption" tells the story of my teen and adult years through the lens of seven issues that are common to many adoptees. Each chapter shows how it is all too easy for adoptees to believe that we are victims of our circumstances. But these chapters also point to the second adoption, a spiritual adoption, that means we are no longer victims but victors through Christ.

"Part 3: Truth that Transforms and Brings Hope" celebrates truth—the truth of the gospel, the truth about the message our culture wants us to believe about adoption, and the hope that truth can bring to all who are adopted into God's family as sons and daughters of the King of Kings.

My prayer while sharing my story is that God will be glorified. I pray that God's faithfulness will be evident and that my story will point to the one to whom we all belong.

> *"But he said to me, 'My grace is sufficient for you, for my power is made perfect in weakness.' Therefore, I will boast all the more gladly of my weaknesses, so that the power of Christ may rest upon me."*[1]

PART 1
THE LEGACY OF
A SPIRITUAL FOUNDATION

My parents' desire in raising their children
was that they would ... never know a day
when they did not know and love Jesus.

CHAPTER 1

GROWING A FAMILY
Bangor, Maine, 1962-1968

For it was you who created my inward parts;
you knit me together in my mother's womb. I
will praise you because I have been remarkably
and wondrously made. Your works are
wondrous, and I know this very well. My bones
were not hidden from you when I was made in
secret, when I was formed in the depths of the
earth. Your eyes saw me when I was formless;
all my days were written in your book and
planned before a single one of them began.
—Psalm 139:13-16 CSB

"There is a child due soon in need of a family and available for adoption. May I refer you?"

One evening in the spring of 1962, my mother received a phone call from a good friend back in her hometown, who told her of a baby coming soon that needed placement. My parents had been filling out applications with adoption agencies and this friend, who had adopted children through private adoption, had been talking with my mother about the process and her experiences.

My parents were excited about the possibility and the wheels were set in motion. Today this sort of adoption would probably not be permitted, but in 1962, things were done differently. Dr. Den Dulk, a doctor in the small town of Escalon, California, helped young women who found themselves pregnant yet unable to care for their child. Dr. Den Dulk would find suitable homes through networks of loving Christian parents who desired children. He had placed a remarkable number of babies this way. I was no exception.

My parents received another phone call a few weeks later. The baby—a little girl—was born on April 14. They could not afford to both fly to California. As my mother was not confident about navigating the legal system on her own, my father boarded a plane to bring me home. He was uncertain about handling a tiny baby on a cross-country flight, but, between friends in California and helpful flight attendants, we made it home.

At that time, my parents lived in Bangor, Maine. They had been married for three years. My mother was 34 and my father was 31 years of age.

My spiritual adoption is tightly woven into my earthly adoption story. My father was a minister in the Orthodox Presbyterian Church (OPC), and my mother had grown up in the Christian Reformed Church (CRC) with a long family history of God's faithfulness going back at least eight generations.

As Christians, my parents desired to have children not only because God tells believers to raise families,[1] but also because the rewards of having children are spoken of throughout the Bible. They had a heart for adoption and desired to have a large family.

My parents started the adoption process after they lost a child midway through pregnancy. I only became aware of this as an adult, because they never talked about it until I had my third child in 1990. Due to serious health complications, I gave birth 26 weeks into my pregnancy. Our tiny daughter Kayla was born weighing only one and a half pounds. My father shared with me that Kayla's size brought back memories of the child they had lost and the sorrow of that time.

My parents believed in the biblical covenant that God made with Abraham, where he promised to be a God to Abraham and to his descendants.[2] This covenant extends both literally to Abraham's offspring and spiritually to all who believe in Jesus's death and resurrection as salvation for their sins.[3] My parents believed that children who belong to believing parents, although born sinful, are children of the heavenly Father through adoption as sons and daughters, just as their parents who believed.

They believed that the sign of this covenant was baptism. Later, when the child was older, they would profess their belief through a public profession of faith in the church, showing God's covenant faithfulness throughout generations.

In his letter to Timothy, the apostle Paul writes, "and you know that from infancy you have known the sacred Scriptures, which are able to give you wisdom for salvation through faith in Christ Jesus."[4] My parents' desire in raising their children was that they would be like Timothy, never knowing a day when they did not know and love the Lord. I am blessed to say that is my testimony.

I was three days old when the adoption papers were signed. Although it took until June to become finalized, there was no question on anyone's part that I was the daughter of George and Grace Haney. They gave me the name Mary Anne. I was called Mary Anne for the first twelve years of my life.

Friends and family celebrated my arrival. I was spoiled rotten … for the next nine months. Yes, shortly after my arrival—as often happens—my parents found out that they were expecting another child. This pregnancy went well and nine-and-a-half months after my birth, my first brother, David Edward Haney, arrived on February 1, 1963.

While I was a chubby and happy baby, David was scrawny and colicky. My mother had her hands full.

She used to tell the story that I was not happy with David's arrival. To show my frustration, I would bang my head against the wall. Concerned that there was something wrong with me, she took me to see the family doctor, who assured her that I would stop when it began to hurt. And I eventually did stop when I did not get the attention I desired. One could assume it also gave me no pleasure.

David turned one at the beginning of February 1964 and I would be turning two in mid-April. My parents decided to write a letter to Dr. Den Dulk expressing their desire for another child.

My mother wrote the letter on her birthday, February 21. To my parents' surprise, they received a phone call the following week with the news that a baby boy was born on February 21. He needed a family and was available for adoption. They immediately said yes.

For the second time, my father made the trip to California, this time to retrieve John Edwin. Before I turned two, I had two younger brothers! With the birth of Stephen Eric in 1966, my parents had four children in four-and-a-half years.

These were busy years as our family grew from a house full of babies to toddlers to young children. Three highchairs lined the kitchen wall, and in the living room there was an oversized wooden playpen that corralled two or three of us at a time.

My father also rigged a traveling playpen that fit in the back seat of the car for longer trips. Car seats were still on the horizon.

Photos show happy, smiling faces of three kids in the bathtub at a time and tricycles lined up on the sidewalk like race cars. When I revisited our childhood home many years later, I wondered how we all fit. But we did—and entertained many guests there as well.

My father pastored a small church in Bangor, Maine, referred to at the time as the "Northeast Outpost"[5] in the OPC. We were there every time the doors opened.

I don't know how my mother managed this, but we were always dressed up in our Sunday best with shoes that were freshly polished the night before. To help my mother out, my father would take one or two of us along to the evening service while my mother stayed home with the baby and one of us.

We three older children were four, three, and two years old, and various scenarios played out at the service depending on who was present. At times, we sat with another family. Sometimes we sat in the front row with the pianist, where my father could keep an eye on us. If we acted up, we were brought up to the front and sat behind the pulpit on a big chair that looked like a throne.

We knew enough to know that, if we were in that position, everyone in the congregation had eyes on us. If we acted out, there would be consequences later. We knew enough to behave.

Growing up in the church was a tremendous privilege. It set the scene for a strong spiritual foundation. We attended Sunday School, heard Bible stories, and memorized songs and Scripture verses. My parents were strong advocates of family devotions. We read the Bible and prayed at every mealtime, even as young children. Is it any wonder that I do not remember a day when I did not know and love Jesus? He was as much a part of my day and evening as my parents and brothers were.

My mother used to tell a story about me from when I was four years old. I was saying my bedtime prayers. When finished, I asked her, "Why do I ask Jesus to forgive me and help me not to sin and then just do the same bad things the next day?" My mother admitted she had the same struggles, to which I replied in shock, "Mommy, do you sin too?"

At this tender age, I realized I had a long road of sinning ahead of me. I also understood that "if we confess our sins, he is faithful and just to forgive us our sins and to cleanse us from all unrighteousness."[6]

My memories of living in Bangor are mostly of snowy winters when my father would dig small caves out of high snowbanks in our driveway. Many surpassed his height of six-and-a-half feet. We loved to play in the snow caves and sit in them to watch the high school kids walk home from the school located behind our house. We still laugh to this day when we think about the chore it must have been for my parents to dress and undress three small children in winter gear for a short time of play in the bitter cold each day. Layers of clothing included extra socks and then bread bags held fast with rubber bands to keep the snow that got inside our boots from getting our socks wet.

My brothers and I also have distinct memories of watching our house on fire. We perched in the neighbor's sink, peeking out her kitchen window as the house burned. The fire was probably much smaller than our memories make it out to be, but it left an indelible impression of an exciting yet scary time, with sirens and lights from the local fire trucks' arrival. The garage and basement sustained most of the damage, but it remains a story that we recall. We all remember sitting in the neighbor's kitchen sink watching the house on fire.

Many of the people from the church became our "aunts" and "uncles," and some families remained lifelong friends. We often used one family's summer camp, a rustic cabin on a lake, and returned to it for many summers after moving away. Those weeks at the lake fueled numerous memories from our growing-up years. The mud that squished between our toes, jumping off the floating dock in the middle of the lake, canoeing, the poison ivy that was inevitable for at least one of us, and the frogs singing at night. They all became a treasure trove of stories to tell each other long after those idyllic days passed.

I began kindergarten while we lived in Maine. A young artist who attended the church painted a portrait of me at this age, and it is one of my treasured possessions. It represents a time of innocence in my life, when I had no worries about who I was or my place in this life I had been given.

I don't look particularly happy in the portrait though. In fact, I cried when the photos used to paint the portrait were taken.

The artist, Ed Healy, was a guest at Sunday dinner—a regular occurrence in our home each week. He asked my parents' permission to paint me, as he was captivated by my dark brown eyes. He later featured the portrait, *Storytime*, on the front of his announcement cards for the opening of his art gallery in downtown Bangor.

The painting itself hung in my parent's home for many years which made me feel special. Eventually I inherited it. When my daughters were young, many people mistook it to portray one of them. It remains in our home today.

I remember being very proud of that portrait as a child. As I got older, I secretly asked the girl in the painting, "Who are you?" I did not feel like I bore any resemblance to the little girl with blond hair and big brown eyes. I wondered what she was thinking and what she knew at that age. I still wonder about that little girl.

Throughout these early years, my parents worked hard to provide a safe and secure home for us. I do not remember much, but I do recall these years as ones when I felt happy and secure. I understood at a young age that I belonged. I was Mary Anne Haney and was secure in my role as a daughter and sister.

In 1968, our family moved from the Northeast to the Midwest, to Menomonee Falls, Wisconsin. My father had accepted the call to help a young church plant become established. We kids were between the ages of two and six and spent our formative years in the young and growing church in the young and growing suburban community outside of Milwaukee.

These were the years when my own identity began to form. These were also the years when the first lie that would pierce my heart wormed its way into the core of my being. I carried that lie as truth for the next five decades.

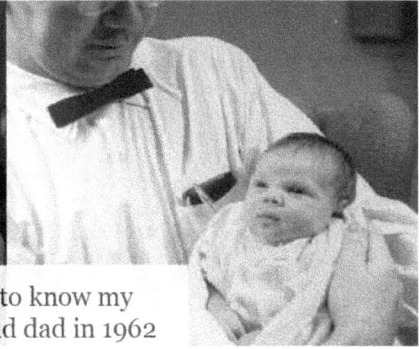

Getting to know my mom and dad in 1962

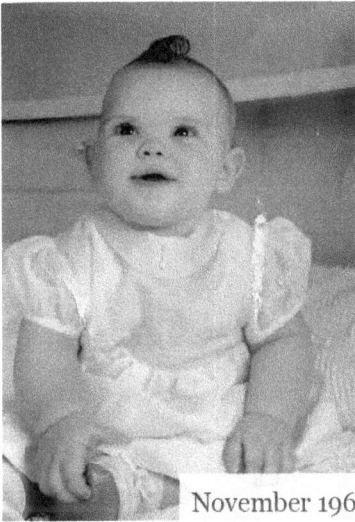

Maine

November 1962

5 years in 1967

Family in 1968

CHAPTER 2

THE FIRST LIE
"I AM UNWANTED"
Menomonee Falls, Wisconsin, 1968-1974

Set a guard, O Lord, over my mouth; keep
watch over the door of my lips!
—Psalm 141:3 ESV

"Sticks and stone may break my bones, but words will
never hurt me." This children's rhyme makes words seem
harmless, but most of us know this is far from the truth.
Words were the first arrow that struck my young heart and
caused much damage.

After our move to Menomonee Falls, I finished
kindergarten at the local elementary school. I don't remember
much aside from nap time on our little plastic mats, the thin
layer of foam between me and the ground.

The next year, I entered first grade at Milwaukee Christian
School in nearby Brookfield. It was a small Christian school
run by the local CRC congregation. First through third grade
was taught in one room with about twenty-five students. Miss
Honadel was my teacher for the next three years. I remember
really liking her. I am pretty sure I enjoyed school overall
because—until I took Algebra in high school—I was a good

student and enjoyed learning. I loved to read and made friends easily with the girls in my class.

The playground was where the first lie happened.

Recess is always a favorite childhood activity and it was no different here, with playground equipment, room to run, and hills for sledding in the winter. The corner of the school building by the flagpole made for a great windbreak on chilly days. But that corner was also the scene for an unfortunate conversation that became permanently etched in my mind.

As our little group of girls huddled in the corner out of the wind, waiting for the recess bell to ring, the conversation turned to the fact that I was adopted. Thinking it had a coolness factor, I shared that I was born in California and my father picked me up in an airplane.

One girl looked at me in horror and exclaimed, "You mean that nobody wanted you?"

Some giggles encouraged her, and she added, "Your real parents thought you were so ugly they put you in a basket and left you on a doorstep."

I don't remember what was said after that. But the image of myself in a basket on a random doorstep remains in my head to this day. The message alarmed me—I was unwanted? Suddenly, being adopted and flying in an airplane as a baby were not cool, unique things to be proud of. The phrase "real parents" was unfamiliar to me and being wanted or unwanted had never occurred to me before. I began to question everything about myself. Who was I? Who were my "other" parents? Why did they not want me? If these unknown people were my "real" parents, who were the mommy and daddy I lived with? This was a lot for a 7-year-old to take in and the questions landed in my mind with a permanency.

On the ride home that afternoon, I asked my father why my "real" parents didn't want me. It must have shocked him to hear my tale from recess—but if there is one thing I know about my father, I am sure he must have taken his time in reassuring me that was not how the story went and to let me know just how much I was wanted and loved.

But the damage was done. My little seven-year-old mind now painted a picture of an ugly baby in a basket on a doorstep, unwanted by the very people who were supposed to love her. This message drilled deep into my heart and I carried the lie for the next five decades. And when you carry a lie for that long, along the way it becomes truth: I was unwanted and given away. I had a mystery family somewhere else that I couldn't know.

Running errands and riding with my dad in our green Chevy station wagon was something I did often. Many of our conversations from those trips are memories I treasure. I know that I was reassured often of my parents' love for me. We talked many times over the years about my adoption and all the things that we did not know about the particulars of my situation. My parents believed and emphasized what we did know: that God in his wisdom had a plan for me to be part of the Haney family.

As a seven-year-old, I did not understand spiritual warfare or how Satan turns thoughtless comments to jabs of insecurity when least expected. It was possibly the first time I understood that perhaps adoption wasn't all loveliness and that, on the other side of the story, was brokenness, hurt and pain.

The thought remained embedded in my mind—that my story was broken, that it contained hurt and pain, and that perhaps I wasn't who I thought I was. In my forties, I would explore this in counseling and would be finally able to articulate the lies that had become a part of my core being. A helpful exercise during counseling was to answer the question, "What would you tell the little girl that just had those hurtful words that she was unwanted thrown at her?" I'd like to imagine that I would wrap that little girl in my arms and remind her just how much she was loved, not only by me, but also by her heavenly Father.

I am confident I was reassured by my parents of their love. But every time I laid down the lie, sooner or later it would spring back to life.

For the rest of the time we lived in Wisconsin, I remained friends with the girl who made those comments. I can still pick her out from a school photo. As an adult, I can see the conversation as the thoughtless childhood comment that it was. But it didn't resolve for me that easily. It became a lie that I firmly believed in the back of my mind: I was unwanted.

Not all of our time in Wisconsin inflicted such spiritual damage. In fact, most of my childhood in Menomonee Falls was innocent and happy, with lots of good memories.

My brothers—first David, then John, and finally Steve— joined me at Milwaukee Christian School over the years and we remained until I was partway through the sixth grade, when we moved again. We, of course, continued to be in church and Sunday School. Many of the songs from those days are committed to memory even now. At school we had Bible curriculum and Scripture memory, and we attended a weekly Awana Club—a program that teaches children about the gospel and emphasizes Bible memory—at a local church. My parents continued their discipline of prayer and family devotions at every meal. Our spiritual formation at this time in our lives was rich and varied.

We had lots of neighborhood kids to play with, and we spent much of our time outdoors. It was an idyllic time of riding bikes and stomping in rain puddles, playing games outside until it grew dark and never fearing for our safety.

A neighbor boy, Jimmy, would come over to play with my brothers. At our house, the rule was we could not leave the table until we had finished devotions. At this stage in our lives, we were learning to memorize hymns, so Jimmy would sit at the back screen door and listen to us singing the hymn of the week. I have often wondered if the songs he heard saturated his brain like they did ours. Jimmy didn't come from a Christian home and often questioned aloud why we were always singing. I am sure it made us hard to forget, at least.

Singing was part of the spiritual legacy my parents were instilling in us. By learning scripture and hymns, we were receiving spiritual training that would remain in our hearts for a lifetime. We knew we were different from many of our friends. It didn't feel like a bad difference; it was just a part of who we were.

Although we kids didn't necessarily think about being witnesses, in hindsight that was exactly what we were. At this tender age, before life became filled with other distractions, we were being taught how to model relational evangelism. When Jimmy asked questions about why we were always singing, we had the opportunity to share of God's love. I don't remember how we answered his and others' questions, but I know the truth behind whatever answers we did give: that our parents were teaching us to hide God's Word in our hearts and to understand the gift of the gospel.

My father had many ideas for how we as children could make a little money. We sold cookies that my mother made, as well as boxes of Christmas cards to our neighbors to earn some money for a long-forgotten project. Neighbors cheerfully cooperated with our little business ventures.

I remember writing and directing a play that all the neighborhood kids participated in. Even the elderly neighbors next door willingly bought a ticket to the show and laughed along with the parents.

I had my first babysitting job at the house across the street from ours. When I heard someone knocking at the door, I called my mother on the phone to see if she could tell me who was at the door. "There is no one at the door," she informed me from where she peered out of our house. But I insisted hysterically that someone was knocking—and even rattling the door handle! My father walked over to investigate, and we were relieved to discover that the ribbons on the front door wreath had wrapped around the door handle and the wind was catching it, scaring me silly. Later I was able to laugh about it.

This was also a period in our lives where we enjoyed many summer family vacations. All six of us would pile into the family car and drive the ten hours across Wisconsin and Iowa to visit family for a whole week. Our family car evolved over the years, from a 1970 Pontiac station wagon with rear-facing back seats to a six-seat Chevrolet Citation that we crowded into as teens and young adults.

We had some rather particular routines for traveling. We would leave early in the morning with breakfast and lunch packed in our vintage Coca-Cola cooler, along with a big jug of water that always sat on the floor under my father's legs while he drove.

Once in the car but before we would leave, we would read Psalm 121. My father referred to this as the "Travel Psalm." As we grew up, we could all recall the words from memory.

On the road, most of us would go back to sleep until our first stop at a rest area. There we would have a quick picnic breakfast. Eating from the little individual cereal boxes and devouring hardboiled eggs were treats reserved for traveling. This process was repeated at a rest stop further along for lunch, where we took a little bit longer to play while my mother made sandwiches from the packed cooler. Then we were on the road again.

Games like license plate alphabet hunts, I Spy, and travel bingo occupied our time. Lots of books were read. Other routines included rotating seats each time we stopped for a break. When we crossed the state line between Wisconsin and Iowa, my mother would break into song with the state song of

Iowa, "You asked which land I love the best, Iowa, O, Iowa."
And, of course, we all boisterously sang along to the song, "M-i-s-s-i-s-s-i-p-p-i" as we crossed the Mississippi River.

There was no air conditioning in cars in those days, so we traveled with the windows down. During one summer trip, David had the front passenger seat while I sat in the back directly behind him. He was tired of chewing his gum, so he removed it from his mouth and—for some reason—threw it out the car window. Yes, that nasty piece of gum blew straight into the back window where I was sleeping. It landed in my hair, where it went unnoticed until our next stop. It had to be cut out of my hair and, although it did not scar me for life despite what my initial reaction indicated, we did have a new rule for travel: No gum may be thrown out the window.

A stop for ice cream in a small country town always rounded out our trip before arriving at my grandparents' home, often in time for supper.

My mother's family lived on farms in the furthest corner of northwest Iowa. Our home base for the week was in the one-light town of Rock Valley. The week spent in that region always included trips to see family members in Doon and Sioux Center, along with those who lived in southeast South Dakota and southwest Minnesota, all within an hour of each other.

My mother came from a large family of nine children. Even though she was the middle child, she was the last to marry. That put us near the bottom of the cousin pack ... and with forty-two cousins, it was a large pack.

We loved our summer week spending time exploring small country towns, playing at each of the family farms, sleepovers with cousins our age, and the occasional job "walking beans" and detasseling corn.

We played outdoor games until it was too dark to see, jumped off stacked barrels on rope swings, and played in hay mows. My grandparents' wooden plank swing could hold a dozen or more people, and splinters in thighs never stopped anyone from jumping on for the ride.

Most evenings there would be a baseball game that a cousin or uncle might be playing in. This was followed by "lunch" at my grandparents' house in town. In this Dutch farming community, meals were named a bit differently. The day started with breakfast followed by coffee time, which was referred to as lunch. This often included a small roll with meat or cheese, along with a sweet treat and coffee. The meal at noon was called dinner and was a hearty meat-and-potatoes meal, followed by a midafternoon lunch, followed by supper—usually a casserole of some sort—then lunch again in the evening. I am sure this kept the farmers who were performing manual labor well fed and energized, but it made the city-dwelling tourists fat.

I can still see the aunts in the kitchen and the uncles in the living room visiting away while the cousins played in the basement or outside. When it was time to gather for goodbyes, the cousins were called upstairs. As many as could fit joined in the kitchen and the rest of us lined up and down the stairs to sing "God Be with You 'Til We Meet Again" and "Blest Be the Tie That Binds," hymns still sung at our Vanden Bosch family reunions today.

My father's side of the family was quite different. He had one sister who was not married until her mid-fifties, so we were the only grandchildren and had no cousins. His family lived in New Jersey near Atlantic City, where he was born. Our trips to New Jersey included time playing in the Atlantic Ocean and lots of card games. My grandfather died when I was six, so it was mostly just my grandmother and aunt, along with any number of my grandmother's brothers and sisters who came to see "Junior" and his family.

My parents had two vastly different upbringings, and we had diverse experiences when visiting with our relatives on either side. But it was always a treat to visit our extended families, and the car trips themselves brought unique family memories.

Soon we would be moving to Philadelphia, Pennsylvania. I don't think any of us realized just how much this change would influence the next phase of our lives. It was like stepping onto another planet.

Family in 1968

Wisconsin

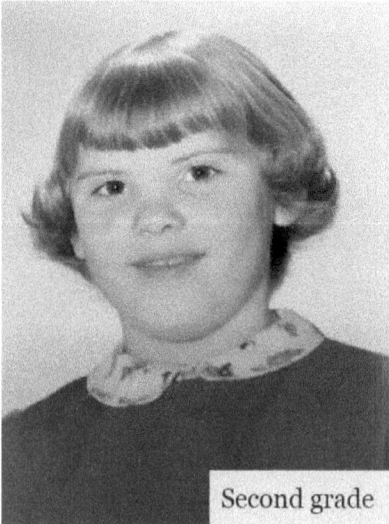
Second grade

Fifth grade

CHAPTER 3

THE SECOND LIE
"HE'S MY BROTHER AND
I HAVE TO HELP HIM"

Roslyn, Pennsylvania, 1974-1980

*Teach me your way, Lord, and I will live by
your truth. Give me an undivided mind to fear
your name. I will praise you with all my heart,
Lord my God, and will honor your name
forever. For your faithful love for me is great,
and you rescue my life from the depths of Sheol
[hell].*

—Psalm 86:11-13 CSB

It's a challenge to be the new kid on the block, especially when you arrive mid-school year to an unfamiliar scene. We felt like country bumpkins arriving at a sophisticated gathering where everyone knew the rules but us.

We moved to Philadelphia in March 1974. We were in for a huge culture shock. There were many contrasts between life in Wisconsin and life in suburban Philadelphia. The demographics were completely different. From a small Midwestern town to a dirty city rich with history. From a new, growing community with young families to an established neighborhood with families that were older and mostly Catholic.

I was in sixth grade, an age when many young teenagers are forming their identity. Phil-Mont Christian Academy, the large K-12 Christian school we started attending, had two sixth-grade classrooms. Each classroom could have fit three-quarters of my entire school back "home" in Wisconsin.

My wardrobe was laughed at. On the first day of school, I was asked, in a rather snide tone, what I was wearing. I was wearing a smock over my shirt that had been made for me by a friend. I had carefully chosen my outfit that morning. And as I got to my classroom and made my way to my seat, I heard a whispered, "Boy are you fat!"

There were many tears during those first weeks of school. I longed to go home to Menomonee Falls.

Even our church was different. Because my father was now in the administration of the denomination and not the pastor of a church, we had options. There were several OPC congregations from which to choose. We settled on one of the larger ones with families that had kids our age, many attending the same school. Several teachers from the school also attended our church, so many faces soon became familiar.

It took time, but eventually we made friends and began to feel more comfortable both at church and school. Friends lived nearby, and we carpooled with them to activities. The church and school offered multiple ways to get involved.

Our spiritual growth during our teen years was no different than our childhood. Between home, church, and school, we studied the Bible, memorized Scripture, and attended catechism and doctrine classes. Our church had a program called Pioneer Girls, with games, activities, and Bible study. Once I graduated from that program, I joined the church's robust youth group, which offered Bible study, music, and activities.

The neighborhood offered a different type of education. That first summer was a revelation.

Our street, Arline Avenue, had a bit of a reputation for being a tough crowd. My naivete showed at every turn. I felt like an imposter. Everything was different and nothing felt right. I did not know where or how to fit in. Barbie dolls were no longer cool. I took no lack of teasing for having them in my room. They were soon boxed up and given away to boost my coolness factor in my attempts at acceptance.

I was introduced to the game Spin the Bottle. My peers played many variations of this game frequently. I learned far more than was necessary for a 12-year-old to know about sex and relationships that first summer. I had my first experience with a cigarette and my first kiss.

It was around this time that I dropped Anne from my name and began to have everyone just call me Mary. There was another Mary Anne in the neighborhood, and it just seemed easier.

One afternoon, a neighborhood mom loaded up as many kids as she could in her station wagon and took us to confession at the local Catholic church down the street. I did not understand what we were doing, but she assured me my parents would not mind. It was my first time inside the door of a Catholic church. I enjoyed its beauty and sophistication from the back row as my friends took turns in the confessionals. I was later told that this was a regular occurrence for the kids on Arline Avenue. However, my parents were not thrilled. I was not invited to go along again.

In fact, that summer was one of the last times I spent much time with the neighborhood kids. Once the school year started again and we began to get more involved in church and school activities, there was not as much time for the neighborhood shenanigans. I would even go so far as to say we operated within a bubble. Our busy schedules did not give us much time for interactions outside of church and school and we had little exposure to the secular world until we began working, with the exception of the occasional contact with neighbors on our street.

My brothers still played street hockey with some of the boys, but the days of listening to music and talking about boys in one of the neighbor girl's bedrooms were over. I made better friends at school and church. I was trying to figure out who I was and what I wanted from life, now that I had choices in front of me.

I do not remember the exact timing of "the announcement," but it was somewhere around the time of my brother John's thirteenth birthday, which would have put me at almost fifteen. It was also the catalyst of the second lie to ingrain into my psyche.

One night at dinner, my father explained to us that when my parents adopted John, they learned that he had the same birth mother that I did. That made us half-siblings.

My parents were so pleased that it worked out that way and saw the hand of God in it. I do not remember how I reacted or responded to it initially. Maybe, deep down inside, I felt a sense of belonging. That was certainly the message that was reinforced at home: "Isn't it great you have each other?" And John seemed to believe that as well.

John had many challenges as a teen and was often in trouble with school, with our parents and even with the law. He continued to struggle with addiction in adulthood. In the 1970s, people were not as open about mental health issues. People did not talk about it and families that struggled often kept their problems to themselves, never sharing information about their struggles with others. John's issues remained undiagnosed until his late twenties and early thirties. And while there were others that knew about his struggles as his reputation proceeded him, we rarely talked about it. It was an unspoken rule that we not talk about any difficulties outside of the home. But within our family circle it seemed that things were always about John. My mother became very codependent on John and was quick to assume that one of us, most often me, could and should help him out.

It was hard to keep track of the incidents involving John. I tried to fly below the radar with my own growing struggles. But the message that I heard with increasing regularity was, "Can you help him? He's your brother, you should understand him."

I believe my parents meant well. They wanted him to succeed. They were admitting that they did not know how to help him. I assume they thought that, since we were close in age, had many of the same friends, and were involved in many of the same activities, I might have special insight into what was causing his behavior.

But Satan is cunning and clever. In my mind, he began to weave messages that I was just like John. It was genetics, we were bad, it was us versus them. And John seemed to buy into the same lie about us. We were special, we were different, but we had each other.

And so I began to believe the second lie: "I am just like him and it is my job to help him." The pressure to help John influenced my thinking throughout much of my young adult life. I could neither escape it by leaving home nor by growing older. Whether at a friend's house as a teenager, at college as a newly fledged adult, or even on vacation with my husband and children, the phone call from my mother would inevitably come. "John's in trouble again. Can you call him? Can you help him?"

Those messages drove a wedge between my parents and myself, especially between my mother and me. Why did I have to drop everything to help him? Why was I responsible for my brother's problems?

It wasn't until much later in my life that I realized my other two brothers felt much the same way: that John was the priority. We all carried resentment for the way he seemed to monopolize our parents and family time.

It took even longer for me to realize that the issue was much bigger than a teenage girl could or should have to solve, even if we did share the same genetics.

But as a teenager, the situation did come with a bright side. The bright side was that John required extra attention, which meant that, if the rest of us were careful, we could keep out of the spotlight. Many times, when John was caught at something, I held my breath and hoped they would not realize I was doing the same things with my friends ... just not getting caught.

And John seemed to get caught a lot.

I have some regrets about my high school years. I wish I had worked harder. I wish that I was not so consumed with shame and guilt, caught in the struggle of "who am I?" and "where do I belong?" I wish I had not been seeking approval from people, rather than God which led me to some dark times of disobedience. I pushed the boundaries on all sides in what I thought was "typical" teenage rebellion. I did not talk openly about what was really going on inside me until I began therapy in my early thirties.

As a teen, the search for my identity was my main struggle. I had many unanswered questions about my adoption and two powerful lies that I thought defined me. I believed that at the root of everything I was unwanted and because of our shared genetics it was my responsibility to help my brother. I fantasized about who my "real" family might be and how things might be different if I had some answers about my adoption. Oddly enough, John was never included in this imaginary "real" family.

I suffered from undiagnosed clinical depression. I literally felt like I had a split personality. I wrote in my journal that there was a "good" Mary and a "bad" Mary. Many people, especially adults in my life, saw the "good" Mary. Adults seemed to like me, and I contributed well to my church and school communities.

But the "bad" Mary lived inside of my head, and I wasn't quite sure I would be accepted if people knew that I struggled emotionally and mentally with who I was and my place in the world. I thought there had to be a reason that I was unwanted. There must be something wrong with me or perhaps I was just a bad person.

Behind the scenes, I was mean and a bully. After one school prank that my friends and I were caught in, the principal called me "the ringleader." While changing clothes for gym, we took a classmate's bra and tossed it toward the ceiling. It got caught in the water pipes that ran across the ceiling, causing laughter on our part and tears on hers. I was ashamed of how we had treated her and knew my behavior was a way to make myself feel better. But it didn't.

I was struggling with anxiety and had countless nights where I could not sleep. I began to have suicidal thoughts no one should be thinking, including, "I just want to die so all the hurt will go away." And I could not talk to anyone about any of it.

But God continually brought into my life people who cared enough to provide the compassion of Jesus. Some of those people had no idea of my internal struggles. They just spoke into my life because it was their call to help young people, and they cared about me. One teacher in particular, Senor Lugo, expressed concern when I fell asleep in class one day. I told him I couldn't sleep at night which prompted a call to my parents, as it was affecting my ability to learn. My mother took me to a doctor to see if there was anything physically wrong with me.

One Sunday, my youth group leader took me aside and asked me how I was really doing and expressed that I seemed angry. I burst into tears, surprising both of us. He encouraged me to talk to him and his wife and this began a time when I started to talk honestly about what was going on in my life. They both invested hours of their time in mentoring me.

At this point, my doctor began treating the symptoms I was experiencing—my headaches, insomnia, even at one point an inexplicable hive-like rash that covered my entire body—but I would not get a specific diagnosis about my clinical depression until college.

When I was finally diagnosed and prescribed medication that helped regulate the hormones that caused depression and panic attacks, I began to see the cycle of depression and anxiety for what it was and what it did to me. But before that clarity, it was a frightening time that I didn't really understand or know how to talk about.

The struggle was not only physical and mental, but also spiritual. And I knew I was fighting a spiritual battle along with my physical and mental symptoms, especially as I reached my later teen years. I was all too familiar with the spirit of darkness that seemed to surround me and knew that Satan wanted me to fail.

It was around this time that I first read *The Pilgrim's Progress* by John Bunyan. The allegorical book fascinated me with its demons and spirits. I could relate to many parts of the journey. I especially understood the scenes at Doubting Castle with the Giant Despair. I felt beat up and not unlike the pile of bones that the pilgrims are shown in the story.[1]

Quotes from the story have impacted me at different times in my life. A personal favorite from Doubting Castle is this one: "What a fool I am! Here I lie in a stinking dungeon when I could be walking in complete liberty! I have a Key in my pocket called Promise that I am sure will open any lock in Doubting Castle."[2]

Another one is from the last chapter, where Hopeful and Christian are crossing the river to the Celestial City. Christian is slipping and fears he will go under. Hopeful's words to him are, "Cheer up my brother, I can feel the bottom, and it is firm."[3] While the story refers to death—and I have witnessed the struggle while at the side of those I have lost to death—I also use this quote to encourage my heart in the dark times of depression. I know I have friends who will cheer me on with the Word of God, and I know that, with Christ by my side in the darkest of times, I stand on solid ground.

Reading *The Pilgrim's Progress* helped me to understand what Scripture says about the dark feelings that plague me and to feel the hope promised in his Word. I still read the book regularly and have even given presentations on it many times over the years.

I also availed myself of many of the books in my father's library. I only wish that in the 1970s there were more topical books available. Today, my personal library is full of Christian authors on the topics of depression, mental health, and spiritual warfare.

Life was not always dark. There were times when things were going well and I was enjoying life, and the dark thoughts from previous days seemed silly. I look back on my high school experiences now with a certain degree of fondness. I genuinely liked my teachers, had a large group of friends, and enjoyed the activities that I pursued, including field hockey, softball, drama, music, and art. I had an active social calendar between church and school. If it were not for the things going on in my head, life would have been ideal.

I wanted to be close to my mother, but we often clashed, mostly over my brother John. She also had strict rules about everything from how I dressed to relationships with boys, and how we treated Sunday. I rebelled against many of them. My father was always available to listen and counsel, but he often traveled, leaving my mother on her own. I remember having some long talks with my father that encouraged me, especially about my relationship with my mother. I tried hard to please her. But I wasn't sure why I didn't please her to begin with.

I was a people-pleaser, trying to win affection. I knew that my parents had enough trouble without me adding to it. I tried my best to keep my mouth shut and my head down.

It worked most of the time. My parents trusted me, perhaps because they were more involved with John and his problems, and did not see the depth of my struggles.

As I moved into adulthood, I carried the first two lies with me—that I was not wanted and that I was like my brother and it was my responsibility to help him.

These lies impacted me in various ways. Sometimes, they were subtle whispers in the back of my mind. Other times, the lies took dramatic action, causing me to make choices that impacted my life in hard ways.

Decades passed before the third lie made its impact.

Family in 1976

1980 graduation from high school

Pennsylvania

John and I as teens

Family in 1981

CHAPTER 4

THE THIRD LIE
"I AM NOT BLOOD"
Manassas, Virginia, 2010

Therefore, if anyone is in Christ, he is a new creation. The old has passed away; behold, the new has come.

—*2 Corinthians 5:17 ESV*

I was an adult when the third lie broke my heart.

More than three decades had passed since my teen years in Philadelphia. Obviously, a lot of living goes on between the ages of eighteen and fifty. I dare say we all hope to be different people as adults than we were as teenagers. Hopefully, the lived experiences and emotional maturity give us a stronger understanding of our autonomy and place. That was the case for me by the time the third lie found me.

In 2010, an aunt passed away. She left her estate to four nephews and nieces, of which I was one. This aunt had been ill for an extended period and, because she had no children of her own, my brother David had been managing her care and her estate. During the final year of her illness, David asked for my assistance on doctor appointments so there would be a woman to assist her. She lived about four hours from me, so the trips turned into overnight stays and I spent some time with her.

After her funeral, we started the process of breaking down and distributing her household goods. She had made some specific requests for various family members and friends, so finding and delivering these items was my brother's responsibility. Several of us volunteered to help.

David had already told me that my aunt's final wishes were for the estate to be split four ways. If we use the number 10, for instance, it was to be split 3, 3, 3, and 1. David and Steve, along with a nephew from the other side of the family, each received 3. I received 1. My brother John did not receive anything.

It is certainly the prerogative of the deceased to choose how to split his or her estate. That is not the issue here. It was a privilege to receive anything. But what happened next caused the third lie about my adoption and place in the family to take root.

My mother, who was aware of the circumstances of the will, asked me how I felt about receiving less than two of my brothers. I should have kept my mouth shut. But, without thinking her question through, I said something to the effect of, "It is what it is, but I wonder why John was left out."

Her response was this: "Well, neither of you are blood, so it makes sense."

My heart and my brain reacted simultaneously. *What?* I am not blood! After all these years, was I still not seen as an equal part of the family by my own mother?

Something deep inside of me cracked. I had to excuse myself and find a private place as anger, grief, and tears enveloped me. I wanted to scream.

Internally, I was devastated. Externally, I had to gain control of my emotions quickly. I did not want this to turn into an emotional battleground without the chance to process the words and the feelings on my own.

I suppressed my feelings until I had the opportunity to process both the statement and my visceral reaction to it. If I looked at it in black and white, I truly did not have the same blood that coursed through my family's veins. But I knew that did not make me any less of a family member. I knew I was an important part of the family. I mattered to the family dynamics. But her statement made me feel like I did not belong.

I fell right back into the belief that I did not belong. My identity, which I thought at this point I had secured, was invalid because of the blood running through my veins.

The three lies flared in my brain: I was not wanted! I was like my brother, so it was my responsibility to help him! I was not blood! These lies were what Satan wanted me to use to define my worth, to create a false identity for me. And I believed his lies. I accepted his false identity of "less than." It caused me great grief.

But God was working in my heart, and he redeemed this crisis of identity into a turning point for me. With a heart softened by the Holy Spirit and maturity that comes with time, I began to realize that these lies were not true. They had no meaning for me nor did they define me.

I belonged. I was worthy. All because of the blood of Jesus and my relationship with my heavenly Father. With the help of a counselor, I was able to define my identity as a child of God and also as a valued member of the Haney family.

Before my mother died, she asked me for my forgiveness for the hurt she had caused me. I willingly gave it, as I knew that forgiveness would bring healing, and to refuse to do so would continue to hold me captive in the lie. Like I forgave my mother, I also needed to forgive myself for letting these lies define me. There was freedom in forgiving myself and for standing in my true identity as a child of God.

A friend, who walked through the hurt and disbelief of the third lie with me, reminded me of my spiritual adoption and how God looks at me. Spiritual adoption is paramount to my understanding of myself as a child of God. Although my mother's words hurt me, they truly did not have any meaning. For all intents and purposes, I was part of this family. More importantly, as a believer, I was a part of God's family, with all the rights and privileges that are included in being an heir. "And if you are Christ's, then you are Abraham's offspring, heirs according to promise."[1]

Spiritual warfare may have held me captive in lies, but the foundational truths were still buried deep inside. And those truths—which flow from the ultimate truth of the gospel—held the power to change my life. This was the legacy of a spiritual foundation that my parents had instilled in me.

While the first two lies affected me for much of my life, this third lie did not live in me for very long. To a certain extent, the first two lies lost their grip on me as well. Thanks to friends and a Christian counselor, I could see the lies for what they were and for what I had made them. They had never truly held the power I had granted them.

The grace of God was never more evident in my life. With the lies no longer defining who I thought I was, I could move forward toward healing. My identity lay secure in Jesus Christ. His love for me defines who I am at my core. It became my joy to search for truths in God's Word that would daily remind me of his love for me and that I was a child of God. I began to fill notebooks again with what I was learning with a changed attitude.

I clung to the truth that in Christ, I was a new person, a new creation. "Therefore, if anyone is in Christ, he is a new creation. The old has passed away; behold, the new has come."[2] I could let go of my past beliefs that I was unwanted and needed to be responsible for my brother's life choices. I could become the person that God promised to make me. The new creation that I desperately longed to be.

This is an active part of the Christian's life—being created new. We are in the continual process of moving forward, even when we are tempted to turn back. The theological term is "sanctification." Even as seasoned, long-established Christians, there is still work to do and we need times of revival and renewal. It is still an ongoing part of my life, but one I now can embrace without past hindrances.

Thankfully, we are not in this alone. Christ walks with us. As I grappled with the third lie, I knew it was time for me to put the past aside and to trust him to carry me forward.

In addition to Christ, fellow Christians walk this journey with us. The Bible refers to fellow believers as brothers and sisters in Christ. Together, as the family of God, those with like-minded faith are here to guide, shepherd, encourage and join us in daily living for Christ.

"Therefore, since we are surrounded by such a great cloud of witnesses, let us throw off everything that hinders and the sin that so easily entangles. And let us run with perseverance the race marked out for us."[3]

Realizing that I had a "great cloud of witnesses" in my friends, those who stood by me to offer hope and encouragement, was a very liberating experience. I no longer needed to keep secret the things that got in the way of growing my faith. Close friends were available to cheer me on in the Christian journey. As the verse in Hebrews declares, we were in the race together. I was not on my own.

The truth was that I had this community all along; I had, in fact, experienced this for many years. Sadly, because I was clinging to the lies that I was not able to openly express, I spent many years overlooking the gift of true fellowship and accountability that God gives us through the church body. I allowed Satan to tell me that I was an imposter, that if people only knew the real me, I would be rejected again. Friendships became far richer as I learned to share my inner struggles.

I don't want to imply that I began to share details of my struggles with anyone who would listen. Some details were too painful to share. But, as I began to see how God had protected me and faithfully led the right people to me, I realized that my story might help someone else. I also began to see that a shared burden holds much less weight than one carried alone.

As I began to see my struggles differently, I also began to see myself differently.

The women's and children's ministries I was involved in became more meaningful when I saw them as a calling from God to encourage the church, rather than activities I thought I *should* be doing. God was gracious to put people in my life who helped acknowledge and affirm my gifts and assisted me in finding meaningful outlets for them.

But many hard-earned lessons—years of being slowly made new—would fall between my teenage life in Philadelphia and the time in my life when I encountered the third lie.

As a teenager and young adult, I encountered some personal and painful challenges. From the time on that playground when I realized that adoption was not a nice, neat package wrapped up in a bow, I struggled with unanswered questions. It was decades before I was able to put a name to my struggle and understand that I was psychologically experiencing an unresolved traumatic loss.

When I found the book, *Seven Core Issues in Adoption and Permanency* by Sharon Kaplan Roszia and Allison Davis Maxon, I saw my experience in the issues that are present throughout the lifetime of the adoptee.

In Part 2 I will expand on the seven themes and show how they played a part in my life as I grew from a teen into adulthood, impacting my beliefs about myself. I will also show how the struggle was redeemed by my faith and the strong spiritual foundation that I received as a child and teen.

As I share my story, I hope to paint a picture of the healing that comes when we give our pain to God, through faith in Christ and in community with other believers. We are not in this struggle alone.

PART 2
HOW SCRIPTURE ANSWERS
THE SEVEN CORE ISSUES
IN ADOPTION

Spiritual Adoption replaces:
Loss with gain
Rejection with acceptance
Shame and guilt with grace
Grief with hope

Spiritual Adoption gives us:
A new identity in Christ
Intimacy with Abba, our heavenly Father
Access to the One who holds all things in control

CHAPTER 5

LOSS

I will not leave you as orphans; I am coming to you.

—John 14:18 CSB

In their book, Seven Core Issues in Adoption and Permanency: A Comprehensive Guide to Promoting Understanding and Healing in Adoption, Foster Care, Kinship Families and Third-Party Reproduction Sharon Kaplan Rozia and Allison Davis Maxon list the first of the seven core issues as loss. "Loss begins the journey."[1]

Loss affects every member of the adoption triad—the birth mother, the adoptive parents, and the child. It also spreads out into the nuclear and extended families.

The adoptee experiences the loss of their birth family, culture, and biological heritage. Loss sets into motion a pathway of other emotional and psychological struggles, which are the remaining six core issues.

Loss continues over the course of a lifetime. Something a person once had is gone. It is missing and cannot be retrieved. A family is separated and a new family is created. Many adoptees, including myself, describe loss as a hole that they don't know how to fill. In many cases, there is confusion as to what that hole is and why it is there.

In her book, The Primal Wound: Understanding the Adopted Child, Nancy Newton Verrier describes in detail the loss an infant feels at birth. For nine months, the child feels and hears her mother. The infant knows every heartbeat, the sound of her voice. The infant is nurtured and soothed by her. This amazing experience, which lasts approximately forty weeks, is "the bonding in utero of the mother and child. Many doctors and psychologists now understand that bonding doesn't begin at birth, but is a continuum of physiological, psychological, and spiritual events which begin in utero and continue throughout the postnatal bonding period. When this natural evolution is interrupted by a postnatal separation from the biological mother, the resultant experience of abandonment and loss is indelibly imprinted upon the unconscious minds of these children, causing that which I call the 'primal wound.'"[2]

For the child to enter the world and suddenly hear and feel her mother no more presents a trauma—an emotional and psychological blow to the infant, who loses everything she has ever known. "That a baby knows its own mother at birth has been proven over and over."[3] To then be placed into the arms of strangers and never feel or hear her mother again, the person she has depended on for everything as long as she has been aware, creates an emotional and psychological trauma that needs acknowledgment and validation to heal. This has become known as the "primal wound."

Learning this horrified me. I had never thought of my birth in that manner. I'd always thought of my life as starting at three days old when my father picked me up and took me home.

The details of the days before my father arrived were not something that entered my brain, nor were they a part of my story. I would eventually meet my birth mother, Hazel, and she filled in more details, but those events still felt like they belonged in someone else's life. My life began when my father picked me up. The rest was too painful to think about and, to this day, does not feel real. It feels hollow.

That fits into the way adoption was experienced at that time. A child was adopted into a family and, from that point on, the child was raised as if they were, in fact, born into that family. The original birth certificate was sealed and locked away. An amended birth certificate with the adoptive parents' names and information as if they had given birth to the child was then produced. This then became the legal official vital record for the child. It was seen as a new beginning, a clean slate. At that time, most adoptions were closed, with no information passed along with the child. To date many states still keep these records sealed and information limited or restricted even for the adult adoptee.

I do not know how old I was when I first experienced a feeling of loss in a physical way. When I would bang my head against the wall as a toddler, the doctor assumed it was a reaction to sharing my world with a brother at such a young age and that I was seeking attention. But maybe it had a deeper meaning. Perhaps I felt the loss of my birth mother even before I could identify and articulate it. We will never know for sure, and to a certain extent it doesn't really matter, but it was the first thing that came to mind when I started researching the issue of loss.

As a teenager, I began to experience an unconscious need to be sad around the time of my birthday. I vividly remember standing at my bedroom window while tears ran down my face. I remember the shade of green paint on the walls and the pink flowered curtains flowing in the breeze. It was a private moment that I didn't share with anyone, but it was repeated many times around my birthday over the years. I found myself longing to know anything about the woman who gave me away.

I was not unhappy with my life; I just had a hole that I
didn't know how to fill. I didn't know why there was a hole or
what was needed to fill the hole so I could move on. Why was
what I had not enough? How could I make it go away? It
would take some time before these questions were answered.

When I was in my thirties, I wrote a letter to my birth
mother. In it, I asked all the questions I had wondered over
the years. I told her all about me. I assured her that I had a
good life and had no regrets about being placed for adoption. I
wanted her to know I was all right. It saddened me that she
had three grandchildren that she would never know and that
would never know her. I told her that I had tried to find her
and failed, but that maybe I would try again someday. I
wanted her to be proud of me by sharing small pieces of my
life with her.

The letter was never mailed, because at the time I didn't
know where to mail it or to whom it should be addressed. This
lonely orphan letter sat in a box under my bed for many years.
But even so, it was a cathartic exercise that brought me some
closure at the time. I had spilled out many thoughts on that
paper, and it cleared out room for new thoughts that could
help me move forward.

The exercise was recommended to me by the counselor I
was seeing at the time. In my thirties, my depression was the
worst it had ever been. I was deeply overcome with grief. My
father was battling cancer, and my youngest daughter was
almost two. We were finally turning some corners on both her
health and mine after her traumatic and stressful birth. It was
the perfect storm of emotions, and several things from my past
surfaced that were troubling for me.

I will always be grateful to my Christian counselor for the
wisdom she imparted at this time, especially on her experience
working with unwed mothers who chose to give up their
babies for adoption. In writing that letter, I was able to find a

new lease on life and a willingness to work toward building a good life for myself and my family.

The opposite of loss is gain. In Colossians 1:9, God tells us all that we have to gain in the Christian life: joy, hope, and purpose.

Christ fills the hole. He takes on the loss we are feeling and fills us with the comfort and hope in knowing that, one day, all will be restored. From him, we gain all wisdom and understanding. From him, we receive redemption and the hope of eternal life.

God's sovereignty and plan for my life included becoming his child through spiritual adoption. In his book, Adopted by God: From Wayward Sinners to Cherished Children, Robert A Peterson shows us how the entire Trinity is involved in our spiritual adoption.[4] The Father loves us and calls us to himself. "We love because he first loved us."[5] The Son redeems us with his blood. "He [Jesus] gave himself for us to redeem us."[6] The Holy Spirit calls us and enables us to believe, confirming our adoption. "Because you are sons, God sent the Spirit of his Son into our hearts, crying Abba, Father!"[7]

But, in spiritual adoption, we don't long for what we've lost or wonder what might have been if only we had stayed in sin, which the Bible calls slavery. The Bible tells us that we strive daily to separate ourselves from our sin and live for the glory of God. Our redemption through the blood of Christ makes us a new creation with new hearts and clear consciences. In spiritual adoption we are redeemed, we become righteous and renewed. In our physical adoptions we might wonder what could be different, or how our stories might be changed? But we don't have to question or wonder in our spiritual adoptions. The answer is before us; we are made new and one day all will be restored. We look forward with anticipation to heaven.

It has struck me more than once while writing this book that looking back and searching for answers from my birth hasn't really served to move me forward. What has helped me move forward is the spiritual training and love from my earthly parents that pointed me to God, who I can call Abba. The Bible uses this word to describe God as our Father, an intimate family name. I gained redemption of my story, and entrance into the family of God, by the blood of Jesus.

Do not misunderstand me. I did keep up the search for, and eventually found, my birth mother and a whole wonderful family that has been very accepting of me and loving toward me. I am richer for it. But while finding my birth mother filled a hole that I had and answered some of my questions, the experience served more to point me to the faithfulness of God and his plan and provision for my life than it did to answer any "what if?" questions. In God's view, there are no "what if?" questions. He plans every one of our days. [8]

But even as I learn to look at my life through God's view, some "what if" questions remain for me on a smaller, earthly scale. When I was given up for adoption, I not only lost a biological family tree, but also the heritage and culture that goes along with that family.

In my thirties, I was obsessed with tracing my adoptive family tree. I was influenced by my father and his search for his roots and enjoyed helping him with his project. I enjoyed telling his story through the many photographs we had available. I also took on finding out as much of the history of my mother's side of the family and telling that story through pictures. Both histories were fascinating to me. It made me wonder what stories I was missing in my biological history.

My adoptive family on my mother's side included an exceptionally large, very Dutch family that was traced back eight generations to the original members who came from the Netherlands. Much of the genealogy work had already been done for us. I loved to read the personal stories and see the photos.

On my mother's side, a family reunion in 2000 resulted in a tally of over 300 direct descendants from my grandparents, including children, grandchildren, and great-grandchildren. I've lost track of the total today, as many great-grandchildren, including my children, have gone on to have children of their own and, in some cases, now grandchildren.

My father's much smaller and very proper family of English and Welsh heritage could be traced back several generations on my father's maternal side. But, as hard as he tried, he could find very little on his paternal side as my grandfather had left home as a teen and would not speak of his family. My paternal grandfather was an avid photographer and had an unusually large collection of photographs beginning in the 1920s, including many of my grandmother as a teen in Atlantic City, New Jersey. These photos fascinated me with the stories they told of a time gone by.

I must admit there was a time when I felt both angry and sad that I could not claim these families as my family of origin. I wanted that heritage to be mine. In one way it was, but I often wondered about the people and stories of my "real" culture and heritage. It seems silly now but I often hoped I came from a story as unique as the one I had adopted as my own.

I mentioned that in a conversation at a family reunion one year, and the responses have always stuck in my mind. Several cousins mentioned they never thought of me as adopted or different from any of them; they always just thought of me as another cousin. One cousin pulled me aside later and told me that he wanted me to know he was thankful God brought me into this family, and that he was glad to call me cousin and especially glad to call me a sister in Christ.

God in his wisdom knew exactly where I belonged.

As an adoptee, it was paramount for me to recognize that the hole I felt throughout my childhood and teen years was real. Understanding traumatic loss and affirming the significance of that loss helped to fill some of the emptiness. We must also acknowledge there is not always a solution to the loss an adoptee feels.

As Christians, rather than embrace the loss as something that will forever define us, we acknowledge that, with Christ, we have everything to gain. He is making all things new. He directs our path, supplies everything we need—including our emotional needs—and promises us that "goodness and mercy shall follow me all the days of my life, and I shall dwell in the house of the Lord forever."9

CHAPTER 6

REJECTION

*Even if my mother and father abandon me, the
Lord cares for me.*
                              —Psalm 27:10 CSB

Rejection is often experienced as a form of social rejection. It is a "perceived loss of social acceptance, group inclusion or a sense of belonging. Rejection can be real, imagined or implied."[1]

An adoptee can feel rejection—or fear rejection—through many ways, including from:

- Birth parents who chose not to raise them.
- Adoptive parents who are unable to bond or form close attachments.
- The stories adoptees make up in their minds when they have no real facts from the loss of their birth family, which often include assumed rejection by the birth parents.
- The question asked by well-meaning people, "Do you know who your 'real' parents are?"

I experienced each of these in some form. "Rejection is stored in memory"[2] and often carries into adulthood. Many adoptees have a heightened sense of fear of rejection from others. This fear prompts unconstructive coping mechanisms, such as ending a relationship first to avoid being hurt if the other person decides to leave. Adoptees with a fear of rejection may also perceive slights that are not there and misinterpret others' actions toward them. Other "manifestations of rejection include self-destructive behaviors such as addictions, domestic violence, poor self-care, isolation, eating disorders, cutting, depression and suicidal ideation."[3]

My daughter Kayla asked me if I really felt like I had been rejected. I had to admit that I did not think of myself as rejected. Maybe the word "abandonment" fit my story better. But I wonder if that was because I still believed the lie that I was unwanted and given away. The fact that an alternate plan had been made for my welfare speaks to the fact that care was taken to give me a future. The word abandonment was later added to the core issues by Marie Dolfi, LCSW, a social worker and speaker who specializes in working with adoption triad members.[4]

My story had always been presented to me in such a way that, when I really thought about my adoption, I felt positive about how God was working to direct my story. I believed, and still do, that my circumstances were ordained by God.

Even then, "fantasies flourish when facts flounder."[5] As I grew up, any number of scenarios went through my mind as I wondered about my history. I didn't know why I was given up for adoption—so perhaps I was rejected or abandoned?

When I was about to turn fifty, circumstances seemed to point me to searching one more time for information about my birth. With help from a friend, I finally followed through on my search for my birth mother and got some answers. Although I had been unsuccessful in previous searches, this time felt right. I was in a healthy emotional place and had the support of my husband John. I was secure in my identity as a wife and mother and felt "ready" for whatever answer I might find.

My Search for My Birth Mother

In November 2011, I was asked to be the featured speaker at a women's retreat in San Francisco. I was presenting, "Journey of a Lifetime: Reflections on The Pilgrim's Progress" to the women of the OPC Presbytery of Northern California and Nevada.

Since the location happened to be close to Escalon, the small town where I was born, I asked my husband, John, if he would come along with me and spend a few days looking around the area. I was slightly nervous about visiting. I wasn't sure if there would be triggers that would set me off emotionally and I wanted his support. But I felt strongly that since we were going to be this close it was now or never to see what we could find.

In God's providence, the trip changed my life in ways I was not expecting. Following the retreat, the local pastor and his wife, Susan, invited us to spend Sunday with them. Susan, who had been the one to invite me to speak at the retreat, was an acquaintance of mine from high school in Philadelphia. She had been adopted too. We had shared our adoption stories with each other as teens. We lost track of each other over time, but we reconnected when she surfaced on Facebook.

As we visited that Sunday, I told her our plans to explore Escalon and the area of my birth. This led the conversation to my previously unsuccessful searches for my birth mother.

Susan had done several successful searches, both for herself and others, and had a good deal of information and resources at her fingertips that I hadn't even known existed. As I shared my story and the few facts I knew about my birth mother, "Hazel," she began to do an internet search.

The first thing we found that evening was that I potentially had a sibling who was a little older than me. This we learned from a newspaper article. A few other pieces of information could be traced to the name of my birth mother, but until some more verification occurred, there was no reason to assume this was the right Hazel.

Susan offered to continue the search on my behalf. I agreed to let her see what she could find, within certain financial limitations. My brother John and I had talked about doing a search together but at this time we were not in communication with each other and I decided to do the search for me. I did not give a second thought as to how some of the information might affect him.

The next day, my husband John and I visited Escalon. We drove past the hospital where I was born. It hadn't been a hospital for a long time—it was a nursing home at the time of our visit. It is amazing what our brains do, though. I felt connected to this place and loved the little town. It reminded me so much of the small country towns in Iowa where I spent childhood family vacations.

A small museum happened to be open on a Monday, and we spent time learning the history of the town and the people in it. I was surprised to see a display on the surname Gustafson, the name on my adoption certificate. I devoured all the information I could find, wondering if I was related to these Gustafsons on which the display focused. It turned out to be a rather common name in the area, so the likelihood was slim.

After the day spent exploring, I was exhausted both emotionally and physically. A few tears were shed on the drive back down to San Francisco to catch our flight home.

When I returned home, I sent Susan everything I had in my adoption file, just in case any of the information was useful. However, very little was pertinent after fifty years. Most of the people and businesses involved no longer existed.

I dealt with a lot of emotions as I waited for information from Susan. I was more excited than anxious this time around. I had searched on my own when I was eighteen, but I hadn't really known how to search and didn't get very far. Keep in mind that at this time the internet was new and most exploration was done by letter and phone. Then, when my kids were young, I tried again and, through my mother's friend in Iowa, got in touch with a nurse who had worked for Dr. Den Dulk back in the '60s. She had helped other adoptees have successful searches, but for me it was a dead end. She explained that most likely it was because Hazel's last name had changed over time. I would find out later this was in fact the case. Again, much of this search was done over the phone. I don't remember being overly disappointed by the results, just resigned that there was no information. Then the internet became readily available and there was information everywhere but sorting through it to find the right information was time consuming. I was thankful that Susan had experience in this type of searching.

When I shared with my mother that I had started another search, her reaction was not positive. She couldn't understand why I felt the need to waste time and money just to be disappointed again. She believed I had all the information I needed.

After that, I decided not to share the search with anyone else so I would not have to deal with negative feedback. I was doing this search for me and no one else and I knew I could handle whatever information I would receive.

I wondered what we might find, but I was also worried that we wouldn't find anything at all. I knew I wanted medical information, but felt intimidated knowing that the search would eventually reach a point of no return. And I was not sure how I would feel if we got to that point.

As Susan narrowed her search further and further, she would ask me, "This may be the last call—do you want me to continue?" I always ended up saying yes.

Six months after our search began, I was preparing to celebrate my fiftieth birthday with a vacation. My bags were packed to go and spend a week with two of my sisters-in-law on St. Simons Island, Georgia. We had all read the series of books by Eugenia Price that took place there and the trip had been on our bucket list for several years.

The day of my birthday, John and I were leaving for the airport to catch my flight when the phone rang.

It was Susan. I explained the situation and asked if I could call her back in a few hours.

"I've found Hazel, so call me back as soon as possible," she said.

Thank goodness for cell phones. I called her back from the car minutes later.

Susan had already spoken to Hazel and had made plans for me to call her. As my schedule for the next twenty-four hours was not conducive to a conversation of this magnitude, I asked her to let Hazel know that I would call her as soon as we checked into our rental house on Sunday evening.

In hindsight, I should have figured something out sooner. My anxiety for the next twenty-four hours was through the roof. I am sure it wasn't any easier on Hazel.

By Sunday evening, I was a bundle of nerves, having already cried several times that day. My sweet sisters-in-law were incredibly supportive and prayed with me before I made the call. They stayed out of sight, but I knew they were eavesdropping, as they couldn't help but be excited for me.

The call went well. Hazel told me that no one in her family knew she had given up a baby for adoption. I had remained a secret for fifty years. I realized that allowing me to contact her was a brave step on her part. She told me that she was going to tell her family about me.

She confirmed that I had an older brother. She told me that, in her situation, she could not support more than one child. She wanted me to have a two-parent family and be able to go to college.

Hazel also told me that she never held me, touched me, or even saw me after I was born. I was shocked. Having given birth myself, I couldn't imagine not seeing the child I had been carrying for nine months. It seemed cold and uncaring to me, until I remembered that, in the 1960s, that's how it was done. It was thought it would make things less painful if no connection was made. She chose that way because she thought it would be easier to leave.

I felt sorry for her and for that baby that went straight into a bassinet. I couldn't even let my mind go there for some time. However, further conversations with Hazel assured me that, while she may not have seen me, that didn't stop her from thinking of me often. She later told me that she called me "Baby Girl" in her thoughts. Even as my birthdays stretched into adulthood, I remained Baby Girl.

She also asked me about my brother John, confirming that she knew we had been placed with the same family. She also confirmed that he had a different father than I did. I told her that he struggled with addiction and that we rarely had contact with each other.

At the end of that first phone call in St. Simons Island, Hazel asked me for pictures and gave me her address to send them. But I wasn't sure if she was open to talking again, or if that was the end. Time would tell and, for that night, it was enough. I had some pieces of my story and the ball was now in my court.

Hazel and I did continue to correspond through mail and phone calls and, a year later, the scene was set to meet in person.

My new half-brother Jim and his wife asked if they could also be present. I brought along my two sisters-in-law who had been with me for that first phone call. We met in Las Vegas, about an hour from Hazel's home in Arizona.

I wrote an article about our first meeting, which was published in *The Gratitude Book Project: Celebrating 365 Days of Gratitude*, edited by Donna Kosick:

> *A young girl walked out of the hospital on a mild spring day. "It's the right thing to do," she whispered to herself as she left her newborn child behind. It was harder than she had imagined, and she was relieved that she hadn't seen or held the baby, knowing how much harder that would have made things. She walked away, resolved that she had made the best decision for everyone involved. She knew she couldn't provide for the child and her young son who was waiting for her at home. She was confident that the family who was adopting her would provide the baby girl with a good life filled with love. "It's the right thing to do," she repeated to herself, "the right thing to do."*
>
> *Decades later, no longer a young girl, she waited anxiously in a hotel lobby. Any minute now, she would meet the child she had given up for adoption. The elevator doors opened, and a woman stepped out.*

*Hazel gasped, "Oh, you are so beautiful!" as
tears filled her eyes.*

*Today is my birthday, and this is my story, told
with love and gratitude that my birth mother,
Hazel, chose to give me an extraordinary life,
including the years of friendship we had at the
end. I will always be grateful.*[6]

After meeting me, Hazel was finally ready to tell her five
sisters about me. She let me know that she wasn't ready to tell
her family that she had given up two babies for adoption, but
that she would tell them about John when the time was right. I
respected that it was her story to tell.

I received a beautiful welcoming letter from her sister Judy
and learned that a cousin lived less than an hour from me.
Shortly after, Hazel and Judy flew out for the wedding of
Judy's grandson, which took place close to where I lived.
While in the area they, along with Judy's husband Leonard,
came for a visit.

Hazel was able to meet my daughters, Lynnette and
Kayla—her granddaughters—although my son Michael and his
wife Laura were living in Japan at the time and missed
meeting her.

When Lynnette's husband Drew entered the room where
we were gathered, he said, "Wow, there's a lot of strong genetic
resemblance here!" Hazel, Lynnette, and I all have very similar
facial features.

John and I also enjoyed a visit to Hazel's home in Arizona.
Jim, Hazel, and I all have April birthdays within a few weeks of
each other, so we got together to celebrate. We spent a day
going through family pictures and I learned some of the
history of Hazel's family. Jim and I also got together several
times, and he filled in many missing pieces of Hazel's story.

Five years later, at Hazel's memorial service, a cousin said to me, "I feel so bad that Aunt Hazel chose to go it alone through that time. I wish we could have all been there to support her."

I too wish she had support. It breaks my heart to think of her returning home empty-handed twice. But I am thankful for the time we had and for the support of her family after I made contact.

I know that Hazel did what she had to do in her situation when she found herself pregnant with me. I was not rejected nor abandoned but, by God's grace, given an extraordinary life—exactly what she wished for me. I will be forever grateful that she chose life for me. I have always been aware that it did not have to be the case.

It can be overwhelming for an adoptee to believe they were rejected or abandoned by the very ones who should love and care for them. That devastation can carry into many different phases and situations throughout the lifetime of the adoptee, often with consequences that are devastating in their own right. What is often overlooked is that placing the child for adoption was possibly the most loving thing that could be done. Relinquishing a child to adoption is never a simple decision and needs to be recognized as such, giving grace to the birth parents because of all the facts we do not know.

It grieves me when I hear people say that God would never break up a family just to make another family whole. This idea is quite prevalent in today's adoption culture. I realize that many people do not understand the effect of sin and brokenness on our lives in this fallen world, nor do they comprehend how God redeems hard situations.

A prevalent question that has been asked through the ages is: "How do bad things happen under the watchful eye of a good God?" I do not attempt to answer that question here. But what I do know and believe with all my heart is that sin and its consequences grieve God. God knows each of our days in advance.[7] His plan is never for harm, but for our good.[8] He is a God who rescues his children.

God has prepared each of our stories to redeem the hard places, heal the broken, and glorify his name. Through spiritual adoption, he gives us a place to always belong, even at our most broken.

Christians find grace and unconditional acceptance in Jesus Christ. When I think back on my adoption and the issue of rejection and abandonment, I take the greatest comfort from a question and answer from the Heidelberg Catechism:

> *Ques. 1. What is thy only comfort in life and death?*
>
> *Ans. That I, with body and soul, both in life and death, am not my own, but belong to my faithful Saviour Jesus Christ, who, with his precious blood, hath fully satisfied for all my sins, and delivered me from all the power of the devil; and so preserves me, that without the will of my heavenly Father, not a hair can fall from my head; yea, that all things must be subservient to my salvation; and therefore, by his Holy Spirit, he also assures me of eternal life, and makes me sincerely willing and ready henceforth to live unto him.[9]*

Belonging to our faithful Savior Jesus Christ is all the Christian needs. I am thankful for his love and faithfulness, his acceptance of me. In him, I have a place where I always belong.

CHAPTER 7

SHAME AND GUILT

I cling to your testimonies, O Lord; let me not be put to shame!

—Psalm 119:31 ESV

"The second spoke in the wheel of *Seven Core Issues in Adoption and Permanency* is shame and guilt, both of which may impact an individual's self-esteem and self-worth and create anxiety."[1] Shame makes us feel bad about ourselves, while guilt makes us feel bad about what we have done.

Shame and guilt connected to my adoption has been a lifelong struggle for me. I felt guilty that I wanted to know more about my birth family and often wondered about them. I felt like this dishonored my parents by not being grateful enough to them or satisfied enough with them.

While there was no doubt in my mind that they were my mom and dad, I still thought about my "other" mother, wondering who she was and what she was doing. It wasn't that my adoptive parents were not enough. I just wanted information—clues that could perhaps fill in some of the blanks.

I also felt guilty spiritually. I believed that God planned my life to include my adoption, and yet I had many doubts and questions about his plan that just wouldn't go away. While I knew that doubt and questions were not sinful, I felt guilty that I wasn't satisfied with my life as it was. I had a good life!

But I wanted to know more and couldn't be completely happy or satisfied until I had more information. It was a nagging guilt and a pattern of not trusting God's plan during this time in my life.

It felt wrong to doubt God's plan, especially when from the outside my life looked great. But on the inside, I was really struggling. Where was this good God who had ordained all my days? As I wrestled with my questions about where I came from and why I was given up for adoption, I wondered if knowing the answers would make my doubt about God's goodness go away. Or would it make me doubt even more? I worried about both options and wondered why I wasn't getting any answers.

My depression caused me great guilt and shame, especially in my teen years when it went undiagnosed and untreated. I felt guilty for wishing my life would end. I knew those thoughts were wrong, but they came unbidden. I wasn't sure where they came from or how to stop them.

I couldn't talk about these struggles, and I didn't even know what I would say if I did. I was very frightened I'd find out there was something terribly wrong with me. I felt overwhelmingly sad and empty. I tried to fill that emptiness with many things.

I look back on my teens as a period where I had a lot of head knowledge from my spiritual formation, but I did not allow my heart to receive it as the peace that passes all understanding. I could spout out the answers, but those truths only reached as far as my mouth and not into the overflow of my heart. I had adopted an attitude of legalism, of Christian life boiling down to being bad or being good and that was how I saw myself.

There was no peace in my soul. Acting out in ways that I knew could hurt me and hurt others was a way to fill a void. I experimented with the typical things that teens find alluring—

alcohol, cigarettes, pushing the limits—only to find that I experienced more guilt and shame for my disobedience.

When I was later diagnosed with clinical depression and came to terms with it as a medical problem, I started to understand the chemical imbalances alongside the mental health issues. I learned how my depression was connected to my headaches and insomnia, and I gained a new perspective.

I even learned to talk about it, although that was many years down the road. And when I did, I felt freedom. Managing my depression became easier when it was no longer cloaked in guilt and shame and silence. By giving it a name and removing the mystery of why I felt like I did, I was able to begin to heal both physically and spiritually.

I am thankful for the advancements in mental health and the openness with which it is now discussed, although I feel sad that it has become such a common problem.

When I found Hazel, I felt guilty that I didn't feel like a daughter. It had seemed of great importance for so long and at first it was exciting and new, but then it wasn't. Life stayed pretty much the same.

So many questions remained, but I felt awkward and didn't know how to ask them. It was almost like dating. I didn't want to do or say the wrong thing. Even as we got to know each other and I felt more confident, I was still cautious, not sure where the relationship was headed.

After the initial excitement of meeting Hazel wore off, I realized with more certainty how grateful I was for my adoption and the family that God gave me. This wasn't a poor reflection on Hazel in the least. I grew to love her in the five years we had together. Getting to know Hazel and Jim, and seeing our similarities and differences, gave me the confidence to live as me, a person with my own unique story and personality.

I learned a lot about myself and found that some of my personality traits were definitely hereditary. Jim had what I would call a "big" personality, and I had often felt like I did too. I was always vocal and often louder than my brothers, who were more matter-of-fact than I was. Growing up, I was often told to settle down. Seeing the same personality on Jim made me realize that it was how I was made. It was different, but it wasn't bad.

There was an easy camaraderie between me and my new brother. A familiarity that came quickly, as if we had always known each other. He felt as much of a brother as the brothers I had grown up with. It was both strange and wonderful to have a "big" brother.

Over those five years, Hazel and I became comfortable with each other and understood each other better, making the relationship easier. But it all took time—and then she was gone.

Hazel passed away in 2017. Her celebration of life was the week after we buried David. Both of those events took place in California, and my husband John and I were able to be part of each of them. It was a difficult and emotional time, but the bright spot was meeting so many of Hazel's family in person. Everyone was so gracious. Although I had been a secret for more than fifty years, they treated me like part of the family.

However, I realized she had not told her family about my brother John. That was an uncomfortable feeling. I had not told John about finding Hazel, so now I was keeping secrets on both sides. I felt so guilty and dishonest.

After Hazel's passing, I lost contact with Jim. I felt guilty about not working harder to keep up with him, but it seemed to be a mutually unspoken agreement to go our separate ways. I enjoy keeping up with my niece and two of Hazel's sisters who have intentionally stayed in my life. Thanks to social media, I also see and hear a lot about cousins and family members that I met.

I never told my mother about finding or meeting Hazel, although I had known her for two years before my mother passed away in 2014. I felt guilty about keeping the news from her, but her reaction to this final search had been so poor that I couldn't bring myself to be hurt by another negative response. I was learning to put boundaries in place to stop what I refer to as "the yo-yo effect"—always wondering if our relationship would remain peaceful or become filled with tension—and it seemed healthier to just move forward without potential changes in our relationship.

Although I told David and Steve about finding Hazel and they were happy for me, I could not bring myself to tell my brother John. Both David and Steve agreed that it was not in John's best interest—partly because he was in prison at the time, and partly because Hazel had not told her family about him. When I told John over the phone several years later, his reaction was anger. He accused me of breaking a promise by not waiting for him. That this was something we should have done together. That I had betrayed him. This kind of anger was a common reaction so it shouldn't have surprised me. He told me to never speak of it again and hung up.

We never have.

When it comes to my brother John, I carried a burden of guilt and shame for a very long time. I felt shame for not including him in the search for my—our—birth mother. It was his story too. But I realized that my story and his story were two different stories, and they did not have to run parallel. We were different people with very different lives, and this search was for and about me. I only had to be responsible for myself and for the information that pertained to me.

Although I am not responsible for him, he is still my brother and, of course, I want him to be safe and to live well.

So many of his choices harmed him physically and mentally, and his relationships within our family suffered. He has good periods when he is a fun and loving brother and uncle. But then the pendulum will swing and he will be in a dark place. We never know for how long.

Many of his choices leave him in dire straits and it saddens me that he often bears tough consequences for those choices. It is hard to think of him in those situations. There have been nights when I sobbed myself to sleep because my imagination would run wild with what might be happening to him.

We love him and we pray for him regularly, but our relationship has suffered and is often nonexistent. My children grew up not knowing him. I felt guilty that I had moved on without him once I was married and had children of my own. I felt like a failure for not being part of a solution for him.

After David's death, I finally realized that it was time to stand up for myself. I finally acknowledged that the guilt I carried regarding John and my inability to help him was unhealthy and unnecessary. After almost sixty years of second-guessing what to do and how to help, it was time to surrender. It was not my guilt or shame to carry any longer.

God in his mercy lifted that burden. He offered me forgiveness for all the times I felt I needed to do what only he can—to save John. I can say with confidence that I laid it all at the foot of the cross and I bear that guilt and shame no more.

I recently came across a song John wrote in 1992. I remember the song from one of the cassette tapes he made for our family. He often recorded music in his Bob Dylanesque voice and even performed in small venues and churches from time to time. This one is called, "Call Upon the Lord."

> *Chorus:*
> *Lord, please forgive my weakness,*
> *Lord, deliver me from this pain,*

Send to me Your grace and mercy,
Lord, I call upon Your name.

Verse 1:
Sometimes when I'm hiding in the shadows
In a cloud of doubt and I know that I'm to blame,
I call out to my loving heavenly Father
And I ask Him, "Lord, please take away my shame."

Verse 2:
When I find myself wrapped up in all my anger
And the guilt of sin is heavy on my mind,
I look to the cross and there I see my Savior—
He died for me, and my sin is left far behind.
That's what I'm saying,

Bridge:
Lord, take away my temptation,
Cover me in your righteousness,
Show me Your salvation,
Lord, let me know Your holiness.

Verse 3:
The Physician didn't come to heal the healthy,
He came to set the prisoner free.
He came to deliver from oppression.
I once was blind, but it's Jesus now I see.
That's why I'm singing,

Lord, please forgive my weakness,
Lord, deliver me from this guilt and shame,
Send to me Your grace and mercy
Lord, I call upon Your name.
(John Haney, May 1992)

The words remind me to remain steadfast in prayer for my brother, trusting that God will provide. And it reminds me that, as sinners, we are not too different from one another, each of us needing God's mercy and his gift of salvation.

How does one remove guilt and shame?

In *Receiving Forgiveness and Dealing with Guilt*, C. John Miller talks about the conscience, which "is God's point of contact to show us our need for him—it's the conscience that helps us recognize our sins, take responsibility for them, and remind us that our deepest need is God's forgiveness."[2]

The conscience is our God-given sense of right and wrong. When we feel guilt or shame, we will get no rest until we examine the cause of the guilt or shame.

Is all guilt and shame sin? Not by any means. Sometimes we carry guilt that is not ours to carry. It becomes a heavy burden. Other times, guilt and shame are reminders that we are, in fact, human. That "in this world you will have trouble."[3]

Depression is one personal cause of grief and shame that is not a sin. Depression is a physical and mental illness. My doctor once asked me, "If you were a diabetic, would you take your medication?" My reply was, "Of course." He then explained to me exactly what my medications did in my body and brain to help with my depression. It all made sense and the shame of needing medication was removed.

Identifying what is sin and what is not is the first step in healing from wounds of adoption. Don't continue to carry a burden that you do not need to. Instead, God calls us to give all of our burdens to him to carry. "Come to me, all who labor and are heavy laden, and I will give you rest. ... For my yoke is easy and my burden is light."[4]

In cases of guilt and shame caused by sin—which, because we are all sinners, we all experience—when we take responsibility to repent and accept the forgiveness God gives us, we can then move on in confidence and free from guilt.

By carrying the guilt of my perceived failures when it came to my brother John, I was sinning. I was telling God, "I can solve this problem myself." Could I? Of course not! Only Christ could heal and save my brother. John's writings confirm that this was his belief as well.

Miller goes on to say, "Christ is the only one with power to forgive our sins. God is perfectly satisfied with you because of Christ's sacrifice of his precious blood."[5]

It can be hard for anyone to release shame and guilt. Shame plays into our self-esteem, how we feel about ourselves. Guilt can destroy us from within when left unresolved. It takes grace to move forward from both. Grace to see ourselves in a positive light when we may feel unloved or unwanted, and grace to forgive not just others but also ourselves when we are wrong or do wrong things.

The grace offered to us through Christ is the solution to this. God is waiting for us to come to him. Mercy and grace are ours through repentance and faith. Guilt and shame can be left at the foot of the cross.

"Therefore the Lord is waiting to show you mercy, and is rising up to show you compassion, for the Lord is a just God. All who wait patiently for him are happy."[6]

"The Lord is waiting to show you mercy." Now that I can take to heart.

Leave that guilt and shame at the foot of the cross. We don't need to carry that burden anymore because "his compassions never fail."[7] Mercy and grace are waiting.

CHAPTER 8

GRIEF

*The one who lives under the protection of the
Most High dwells in the shadow of the
Almighty. ... He will cover you with his feathers;
you will take refuge under his wings.
His faithfulness will be a protective shield. ... I
will satisfy him with a long life
and show him my salvation.*
                                        —*Psalm 91:1, 4, 16 CSB*

"Grief is the gateway to healing."[1] Important to the healing
process is acknowledging our losses and realizing that grief
can be messy and hard. It is labor intensive, and it can feel
never-ending. Understanding this is the first step in working
through our grief.

Our culture has few models for healthy grieving and very
few of us have been taught how to cope with loss. While there
are universally accepted stages of grief, it is an individual
experience and cannot be defined by time or experience.
Adoptees need to be aware of the ways grief presents itself in
our stories. Grief can tempt us to doubt the goodness of God.
It can also make us angry, anxious, and alone, and can even
lead to deep depression.

Did my depression stem from grief related to my adoption?
Hazel took the question a step further, asking me one time: "Is
it my fault you lived with so much depression?" I assured her it

was not her fault. At the time, I wasn't sure what role my adoption played. Now I understand more about grief, trauma, and their impacts.

For the Christian, the antidote to grief is the hope that Christ provides. Not only does he promise us eternal life, he also promises to return one day to remove all sin, suffering, and death. At that time, he will gather all of his children into his presence forever. It will be a joyful time for those who know him. As we wait for that day, we have many questions that do not have ready answers. But our hope remains in Christ, who makes all things new.[2]

What did I grieve as an adoptee?

- I grieved the lack of information. Who were those people who gave me up? Where were they? What was their life like?
- I grieved not knowing why I was unwanted. What happened that I had to be adopted?
- I grieved not being able to help my brother John.
- I grieved not being able to love in full capacity. What was wrong with me?
- I grieved the hole left by the loss caused by my adoption. Why did God do this to me? Why could I not be secure in who I was? And why did these thoughts plague me at the most inopportune times?
- I grieved when I had a child that Hazel did not know this beautiful baby.
- I grieved that my children would never know this person who influenced their genetics, contributed to their looks and personalities.
- I grieved the unknown answers to questions I could barely articulate.

But I never did anything with that grief but deny it. I told myself to stop it. I believed it was silly to let it take over my thoughts and emotions. And yet, I couldn't make it go away.

I felt tremendous guilt—I was happy in the family God had given me and whom I loved, so why couldn't I stop grieving?

In *The Body Keeps the Score*, psychiatrist Bessel Van der Kolk wrote about the connection between brain, mind, and body in how a person responds to a traumatic event. To broadly sum up his scientific findings, when we suffer loss, it affects not just our emotions but also our body and mind. When we do not deal with the pain of that loss, it can manifest in a myriad of ways, including physically, mentally, emotionally, and spiritually.[3]

And I did not deal with it. As a child, I developed the habit of figuratively stuffing my grief into a little box of my own making. I packed it away and locked the box shut so I could function. I could pretend all was well, as long as there was room in the box for more.

But eventually, as I packed more and more into that little box, it became very full. It began to spill out. My anxiety, headaches, sleeplessness, and anger began as early as middle school. I also stuffed those deep down inside. Eventually, the box exploded into depression and thoughts of suicide.

Our bodies really do permanently absorb what is happening to us emotionally, physically, and spiritually.

Physically, I was exhausted, yet I could not sleep. My chronic, debilitating headaches were eventually diagnosed as migraines. I have struggled with them through the entirety of my adult life.

Emotionally, I hated my body and struggled with food, beginning to cycle through a variety of unhealthy eating habits. I was anxious, unsure where I belonged, and trying so hard to fit into specific social groups, always worried that I could be rejected at any point. I was constantly angry at myself and others, which manifested itself in poor behavior both at home and school: picking fights, being manipulative, bullying, and playing the constant mind game of comparison.

Spiritually, I was afraid and full of doubt. Would God abandon me too? Was I sinning by having suicidal thoughts? What would happen if I followed through? How could I get these thoughts to stop? Why could I not find solace in God's Word? I felt as if there were two sides to me: "good Mary," who was known to most people, and "bad Mary," who lived inside my head.

The Bible tells us that we are created in the image of God.[4] "We are created with a mind, soul, and body. Each part of us was created by God intentionally and is part of what makes each of us who we are. We should see our whole self—spiritual, emotional, and physical—as created with a purpose and inherent value because of who we are as God's image bearers."[5]

But I did not see myself that way. Instead, I saw myself as a failure, as unwanted and unworthy. As I progressed through high school, I began to treat my body, my mind, and my spirit exactly as I saw myself. On the outside, I maintained a façade of normalcy, but on the inside, I was screaming for acknowledgment that all was not as it should be. I needed help.

It took almost a decade to get the help I needed.

As I look back, I see the goodness of God during this time. He placed specific friends and some adults in my life who I felt were safe to let in to small bits and pieces of my life. In particular, my friend Gayle spent countless hours listening to me and loving me as I was, modeling for me what a godly woman looks like and showing me through her example and Scripture where to find answers to my hard questions. She and her husband Richard have spent many hours over the years counseling me, first by myself and later with my husband as we prepared for marriage and beyond. What a privilege to have lifelong friends who point you to Jesus through many challenges and blessings.

One Scripture became very special to me:

"When you pass through the waters, I will be with you; and through the rivers, they shall not overwhelm you; when you walk through fire you shall not be burned, and the flame shall not consume you."[6]

Other seasons of grief also affected me as an adult. My parents died. David died. And John disappeared.

The dates and years of problems surrounding my brother John have blended as our family has gone through his battle with addictions. His story is not my story to tell, but how I have been affected as his older sibling is my story. The lies surrounding that truth held me captive for years.

And one of the most significant parts of that story is when John disappeared.

We went for months not knowing where he was or if he was even alive. During this time, I was in deep despair for his life and completely helpless to do anything. Psalm 91 became my comfort, where we are given the picture of safety and refuge under the Almighty's wings and the words "his faithfulness will be a protective shield."[7]

I also grieved that I had ever believed the lie that I was the one to help him—so much time wasted and life complicated by the belief that, because we shared a bloodline, I was responsible.

Each of these griefs triggered physical, mental, and emotional responses that spiraled down into depression. In God's providence, spiritual counseling was available to keep the depression from turning to destruction. Fortunately, by this time, I was mature enough to know when I needed to seek counseling and did just that, along with medication adjustments when needed.

My father's death was particularly hard. He was our rock. His calm demeanor blessed our family with a sense of peace, even when things were not particularly peaceful. Two years before he died, I wrote him a birthday letter, which later became the words I spoke at his funeral.

Dear Dad,

Happy Birthday! Allow me to brag on you for a few moments. I know your humble spirit will chafe at my words, but it is your birthday, after all, and a personal letter should far outweigh a Hallmark card.

Dad, I think back to our first days together. It was an unusual time for a father to be alone with his newborn child and an airplane was an unusual place to bond together. I can imagine you were nervous about your lack of experience with diapers and bottles. But I have seen how you handle your infant grandchildren, and I know I was looked at with love and treated with gentle care. You brought me home to begin our family and I am forever thankful to our heavenly Father who chose to place me in your arms.

As I work with snapshots in my many photo albums I see glimpses of our life together. Pictures from different stages of my life show your love and pride in me as your daughter. My favorite is the one from my wedding where you walk me down the aisle. The look in your eyes shows your delight in me, and I am grateful to see that same look in pictures throughout my life. Thank you for loving me well, with love and pride.

Some of my fondest memories are the times we spent together shopping for mom's birthday and Christmas presents. Do you know how important you made me feel? Another special time was the car trips we took together, especially the trip to Covenant College. This was a very difficult time for me and yet you listened without judgment—placing value on me and allowing me space to grow.

I remember a letter you wrote to me at college after I asked a question about quiet times with the Lord. Thank you for encouraging me to use music as a tool for my times with the Lord. To this day, music still plays a large part in my walk with the Lord. It soothes. It heals. It expresses words of praise and adoration when I can't, and it quiets my heart. Music has been used to teach our children of God's love and his ways and I still sing to my children each night. They have each chosen a song that reflects their walk with the Lord, and they still love to hear it sung. What a legacy you began with a few simple words directing me to my heavenly Father.

As I reflect on your ministry, I want to thank you and mom for the many sacrifices you both made. Sacrificial giving and a servant's heart just begin to sum up all you have done for our family and for the kingdom of God. Watching you meet challenges in your life and ministry encourages me to remain faithful in my own call from the Lord as you point me to my heavenly Father.

Dad, for seven years now we have watched you battle cancer and the demons of terminal illness. You have been so faithful! Still working for the Lord in whatever capacity is needed, never complaining or allowing Satan to have his way with your spirit. You have remained faithful and filled with praise for what the Lord is doing. What a testimony this has been to those around you as you show us what it means to be joyful in affliction. You continue to point us to the giver of all good gifts.

Thank you for sharing with me the times that you and mom pray for us and our children. It is a blessing to know that every morning you take us before the throne of grace. It was such a blessing to share in that time on our last visit with you. How wonderful to know that each day you pray for me by name. God has answered those prayers in many ways over the years. Your faith is made evident in answered prayer and in the things yet unseen. Thank you for taking me before our heavenly Father.

How can I begin to thank you for the years of guidance and appreciate you properly for the influence you have had in my life? I can be thankful to God, who in his infinite wisdom chose you to be my earthly father so that I might be privileged to see glimpses of my heavenly Father.

I love you Dad,
Mary Anne
July 28, 1997

One thing I gained through adoption was a father. There are no records, not even the name, of my biological father. The only father I ever had here on earth represented my heavenly Father well.

My mother died fifteen years later in a hospice facility in Lancaster, Pennsylvania, in 2014. I remember the grief I felt at my mother's passing. We had our moment in the hospital where we sought each other's forgiveness for the times we had sinned against each other in our words and actions, but I still felt a tremendous loss and deep regret that the closeness I desired had always seemed to evade our relationship.

After her death, David, Steve, and I took care of the items that needed immediate attention and said our goodbyes. We each left to travel back to our homes in different states on the East Coast.

Complicated by the grief of her passing was the need to get word to our brother John, who was then an inmate in a Michigan penitentiary. Admittedly, I was angry that—on top of everything else—we had to figure out how to include John in the plans for her funeral, even if it just meant calling him so he had someone to talk to. And I did not want to talk to him. But my mother had such a hard time letting go because of his situation. Before she passed, we children had each promised her that we would do everything we could to support him.

I left the hospice facility with this turmoil in my mind. The thoughts played over and over as I began the four-hour drive home to Virginia.

About halfway home, I let out an involuntary moan that grew in intensity until it overflowed into angry tears. The words spilled out of me: "No, no, no!"

Tears blurring my vision, I exited the interstate, pulling into a parking lot, and cried uncontrollably for several minutes. I could not stop the sobbing of my broken heart for all the times John's needs took precedence over ours.

When I was finally calm, I walked around the parking lot until I was ready to continue the drive home.

Forever etched in my mind will be the iPad that sat on the front pew with us at our mother's memorial service as it livestreamed to a prison room, where John sat with a pastor so he could be a part of the service.

I could not go to the front to speak that day, unsure if I would be able to maintain control. But there was much I wanted to say about the woman I called mom.

Her favorite song was "Great is Thy Faithfulness" and we sang it often. She always had a song in her heart and sang loudly from the front of the church.

"After her death, her confidence in God's faithfulness continues as her testimony and legacy to the church. Through difficult times, she knew that God's mercies were both new every morning and sufficient for every dark night."[8]

My mother took hospitality very seriously. There were very few Sundays when we did not have a table full of guests for dinner. Her table had guests from around the world. She wanted to be a missionary before meeting my father, but God closed those doors for her. So, she made her home a mission field, teaching immigrants English by reading the Bible with them and writing letters to prisoners as part of a Bible Study program for inmates.

She was a hard worker, passing her work ethic on to her kids. Every summer we would make trips over the bridge from Philadelphia to New Jersey—the Garden State—where we would bring home the bounty of whatever was in season: strawberries, tomatoes, cucumbers, corn, green beans, apples. Everyone was given a job. We worked all day to "put up" the harvest for the year to come.

I remember her still hard at work canning in her seventies and making jam in her eighties. I recall sitting in her living room in Virginia, weeks away from giving birth to my son, snapping beans while she handled hot jars in the kitchen.

As she aged, she spent a lot of time in her recliner. Stacked near her was her well-worn Bible, detailed notes in every margin, a devotional book, a prayer guide, and materials for correspondence. She spent the better part of the morning in that chair worshipping God and encouraging others.

Throughout the homes of her children and grandchildren and many friends, you will find elaborate cross stitch works, all made with love. We lost count of how many she finished, but they remain a beautiful reminder of her love.

As we grow older and watch our parents age, we realize that at some point we will be without them. It is a natural end to life. What catches us by surprise is the loss of someone whom we assume has many years of living still ahead. That was the case for our family when David unexpectedly passed away at the age of fifty-six.

It was a shock to the community at large. Many of us were in denial, finding it hard to believe that he could be gone. It seemed surreal that someone who played an important role in our family was no longer with us.

David and I enjoyed a close familial bond. We regularly talked on the phone during his commutes, and our families visited together when possible. We worked together on several family issues, including caregiving for our parents and other family members. He had walked through hard times with me in relation to our mother and our brother John. He had been the rock our family needed after my father passed away.

A few years before he passed, we talked about my adoption. He told me that he never really thought much about it. To him, I had always been his sister.

His passing was a profound loss and continues to leave a large hole in our lives. I will always miss him.

Grieving those we have lost means that we have loved. I loved my adoptive family deeply and was loved by them in return. Grieving takes on all kinds of forms and there is no rule to tell us what or how to grieve, or even how long it will take. As I have learned, grieving is necessary for a healthy life. Denying grief can only harm us in body, mind, and soul.

Most adoptees grieve not only the loss of the family who loves them, but also many unknowns. Denying the grief of the unknown does not move us toward healthy growth and stability. But to sit in our grief with no place to go with it becomes problematic.

Christ calls us to give him our burdens and he will care for us.9 And the Christian does not grieve without hope. Someday we will be reunited with our loved ones. Someday we will have answers to all of our questions. And we are promised no more sorrow or tears.

I eagerly anticipate that day.

CHAPTER 9

IDENTITY

But now thus says the Lord, he who created you,
O Jacob, he who formed you, O Israel: "Fear
not, for I have redeemed you; I have called you
by name, you are mine."

—*Isaiah 43:1 ESV*

"Identity is the fourth spoke in the wheel. Every individual is on a quest to understand who they are and where they fit— their reason for being."[1]

Identity, how a person views themselves, is formed in relationships with other people, because humans are "social, emotional beings built to live in meaningful connections within our family and clan."[2] When adoptees are missing parts of their stories, up to and including actual people, they may view their identity as incomplete.[3]

"The last three core issues are focused on creating empowerment and healing; it is a shift from losses to gains."[4] If the adoptee has not dealt with the first four core issues— loss, rejection, shame and guilt, and grief—challenges with identity may occur.

As is true with most adolescents, my struggles with identity, who I was, and my place in this world, reached a peak in my teen years. Believing the lies that I was unwanted and that it was my responsibility to help John in his struggles took their toll on me. My depression and my physical symptoms from the stress of emotional challenges set in.

Although my parents were diligent in seeking out medical attention for my problems—my headaches, insomnia, and hives—they were treated as physical problems, not symptoms stemming from psychological issues. While they were much later resolved with simple vitamin injections and counseling, as a teen these problems led to sleep deprivation, anxiety, and even more severe headaches. They caused me to miss school, and my grades dropped because I could not focus.

I suffered because I insisted on keeping my physical and psychological distress secret. I kept putting up a good front because I believed if I acted as I thought was expected of me, I would be well-thought-of and liked—the identity that I was hoping for. I played field hockey, got parts in the annual school musical, and sang in the school's choir and Madrigal Singers. I even soloed on occasion. I stayed active in the church youth group and had many friends. But on the inside, I was miserable. I was making choices that were self-destructive, such as drinking and smoking, because I thought it helped me to fit in better with my peers.

My identity when I was with my family or at activities continued to be the "good" Mary, an involved student and a friend to many. The "bad" Mary showed up on the weekends when it was more important to conform to the group—but come Sunday, "good" Mary needed to be back again.

Throw in a liberal dose of trying to keep my brother out of trouble, and I got very confused about who I was supposed to be.

It all culminated in a disastrous first semester at college, where I could no longer keep up with my studies, job, and activities. I quit after the first semester and went home. I was devastated to be what I considered a complete failure.

Home was not a good solution either. I was completely lost and unsure of my role.

I was hired at the nonprofit I had worked for the previous summer. The organization ran summer camps in the city for underprivileged children from the surrounding neighborhoods. My job was planning and preparing for the upcoming summer camps, including teaching some older camp counselors how to drive school buses.

Yes, believe it or not—at nineteen, I was experienced in driving school buses, including using a double clutch, and had driven all over Philadelphia the previous summer taking kids on field trips to the zoo, baseball games, and historic sights.

However, the young men I was training were all older than me and were not as appreciative of my experience. The racial slur "white b—tch" was often tossed my way, followed by laughter and innuendos.

I was uncomfortable, but I didn't want to lose my job. So, I laughed along and treated them like buddies. I was young and naïve. I continued to use alcohol and other destructive behaviors to numb the pain.

As you can imagine, this did not end well. Their harassment eventually led to assault.

I was more confused than ever. I worried what people would think about me if I failed again. I stayed at the job despite the circumstances, keeping the assault a secret, continuing in denial that anything was seriously wrong. I did not like the person I had become, but I did not know how to change. In hindsight, I knew what I should do to change. But it seemed too hard. I feared rejection. I feared I would lose everything. Somedays, I did not want to get out of bed.

It all came down to one thing: I did not want to be me. Thoughts of ending my life were strong. Ironically, it was the thought that this would be the ultimate failure that kept me from doing anything.

There were some bright spots during this time. Several of my high school friends were also home and either working or going to college locally, so I had options for ways to spend my time outside of work. By midsummer, I was going to a party every weekend.

Around the same time, my father encouraged me to make plans for the fall and suggested I explore the possibilities at Covenant College, a Christian college on Lookout Mountain, Georgia. I think he knew far more about my activities than I gave him credit.

By August, he was insistent that I needed a plan. I applied to Covenant at the last minute, was accepted, and found myself packing to go off to school once again. I didn't want to go but I also did not want to stay at home.

Nothing had been resolved with my health or my mental state. In fact, the harassment I had endured and the party culture in which I had participated turned my teenage angst into bitterness and resentment against everyone, including God.

Looking back, my father must have known how badly I needed the culture of accountability that college provided. I know my parents were praying that I would find my way back to peace with God.

My father drove me down to Lookout Mountain. I don't remember the entirety of the conversation we had during the trip, but I do remember him urging me to find my footing in Christ, to focus on all that I knew to be good and true, and to seek answers through Bible study and prayer. He encouraged me to want to know more, to explore deeper into my faith. He shared with me his own story of coming to Christ as a teen and how it changed his life trajectory in college.

The conversation was a turning point for me spiritually. With my father's words echoing in my head, I was determined to do better. I searched for God's calling on my life. I knew I did not want to continue in the path I had carved out for myself back home, but I didn't know what I *did* want to do.

A central theme at Covenant revolved around our identity in Christ, searching out who God was calling us to be. This resonated with me as I wrestled with finding the identity God wanted for me instead of who I thought I should be.

In particular, I remember a sociology class on family that I really enjoyed. It was nice to ask questions that could be answered instead of the ones that might never be answered. I wrote a paper for this class on being adopted that got me a good grade and an invitation for a discussion with the professor. It was a time of switching my thinking to what I did know, rather than focusing on what I didn't.

I got involved in a local church, began a time of daily quiet times, and attended a Bible study on campus. These activities were an important part of beginning to make better choices for myself, even though there were still many temptations at a strict, conservative Christian college. Temptations that I fell for on more than one occasion.

My father had promised me that, if I wrote a letter home each week, he would send me ten dollars. "Pin money," he called it. Those letters and the weekly phone calls kept me on my toes. I wanted to please him. And I did not want to fail again.

Hope was on the way. At the end of my first year of college, I was invited to live with a family for which I regularly babysat. They were expecting their fourth child and offered their guest room to me in exchange for help with their busy family. I was an early childhood education major, so this was a perfect fit. The guidelines were almost too good to be true: I was able to keep my work-study job in the kitchen at school, so most days I was at school from eight in the morning to three in the afternoon and was home for the rest of the day and early evening as a mother's helper, followed by studying at night.

Another highlight was buying my first car, as I needed transportation since I was not living on campus. I loved my cherry red Chevy Nova and I loved living off campus. As I experienced more independence, I began to want to be responsible for making good choices for myself. I was not always successful, but I was making progress.

Being part of a family was a balm to my soul. I was encouraged to bring friends home and the kids loved the attention they received. This family and I remain close to this day.

Shortly after the fall semester started, I was introduced to the man who would become my husband: John Underwood.

I knew about John because he also worked in the kitchen but I'd never actually met him. He was also on the basketball team and I had attended several of their games with friends. A mutual friend I'd known since high school back home, who was also a basketball player, introduced us one day at lunch. We struck up a conversation, hit it off, and within a few weeks went on our first date.

While the date itself was not memorable, what we both do remember was how we fell into effortless conversation in front of his dorm and talked nonstop for hours until a security guard knocked on the window of my car and asked us to move on. We laughed, said goodnight, and I drove home knowing I'd found a really solid guy.

We scheduled as many kitchen work hours together as we could and, although that semester was busy with basketball and childcare, we found as much time to spend together as we could. In fact, most of our dates were basketball games and babysitting.

We had two opportunities that school year to travel home to Vienna, Virginia, where my parents now resided. They met John early on in our relationship and were delighted by the way he cared for me and the camaraderie of our relationship.

In a very telling letter I received from my mother, she wrote how much she and my father liked John. She specifically wrote they felt he had a calming effect on me and I was a much easier person to be around. After my grandmother met John in the spring, she wrote me a letter with almost identical wording. Suffice it to say the women in my life were very pleased with "my young man."

Although I credit John for softening me, I also believe that this relationship was different from past relationships because I had started to like myself. I was finding an identity that suited me. It had nothing to do with old baggage of where I came from and everything to do with the life I was making for myself, with the love of a man and the unending gracious love of God.

In the spring of 1983, I completed my student teaching assignment at a preschool in the inner city of Chattanooga, Tennessee, and graduated with an associate of arts degree. Following graduation, John went home to Iowa and I went back to Philadelphia for the summer where I had been offered a job. Although my parents had moved to Virginia to pastor a church, I knew no one there and preferred to be with my friends in Pennsylvania. I lived with friends and worked at the OPC headquarters, performing data entry for Great Commission Publications.

One of my first phone calls from John contained disheartening news. The summer job he had gone home to work wasn't going to pan out. He didn't know what he would do if he couldn't find something else. He was discouraged by the lack of jobs that summer and was worried he wouldn't be able to return to college for his senior year.

That weekend, as I visited my parents in Virginia, I reiterated that phone call to my father. Long story short, John had a job in Virginia within the week and moved into my parents' basement.

Unknown to us at the time, that job would turn into John's lifetime career. Eventually, he would own the company that saved his summer and his education.

That Memorial Day, we became engaged and within a month I moved back to Virginia to care for my grandmother, who had also moved in with my parents. We decided on a December wedding, after which we'd move to Lookout Mountain so John could finish his last semester of college at Covenant while I worked at the preschool in Chattanooga.

For the first time, I felt excited for my future.

Before the summer ended, we drove out to Iowa to meet his family. John was one of eleven children ranging in age from eleven to twenty-seven. His parents had farmed in eastern Iowa their entire lives and the family was very involved in the local church and Christian school. I was looking forward to being part of a large family.

From there, we traveled to Northwest Iowa for a few days and I introduced John to my extended family. My aunts and cousins surprised me with my first bridal shower. This began a fun season of showers, introductions to friends and family, and other pre-wedding activities. Life became rich and full of new friends and future plans.

We were married on December 30, 1983. We spent our honeymoon setting up the little cabin on Lookout Mountain that we would call home until John's graduation. It was charming and cozy with stunning views. We could not have been happier.

This story—from feeling like a failure after dropping out of college to settling into my new home with my new husband—spanned about three years. I marvel how God in his wisdom orchestrated our lives by placing specific people in them at specific times when we needed them most. Or how these people, all strangers in the beginning, would become family to us over time.

Adoption culture tends to paint adoptees as victims of their circumstances, their relinquishment, their placement, and the unanswered questions in their lives. And it is so easy to become consumed by our hard circumstances, both real and imagined. We quickly forget how God feels about us when we let our insecurities and our self-imposed labels define our identities. Scripture shows us that we were created to be victorious, not victims. God is for us, not against us.[5]

Our salvation is a transformational part of our identity. The picture Scripture paints of spiritual adoption is simple. As his, the Christian is identified as a child of God: beloved, friend, and heir. That is how God feels about us.

My identity is not in a bloodline or a culture, or even in my talents and abilities. My identity is simply in God's purpose for my life.

But Satan doesn't want us to succeed with the plan God has for us. He wants to steal our identity as a beloved child of God and keep us in a place of doubt about God and his goodness. His goal is to keep us insecure about who we are and our place in God's plan. Satan wants to convince us that we could have something better.

But God gives us everything—there is no reason to look for something better. Even the hard times are times of his care and instruction for us, if we will only listen and observe what he is doing.

So many of my circumstances during this period were a result of bad choices I made. They had nothing to do with my identity. I was not a victim of my choices. I was not defined by my health challenges, my depression, or my failures. I was a sinner, yes, but a sinner saved by grace and forgiven by the blood of the Lamb.

I was identified as a child of God. Because of grace, my identity rests in him.

Like everyone else, the adoptee must be sure that, as they search for their identity, they are searching in the right place. Who and what are we using to define who we are and our place in this world? At certain points in my life, I used the wrong measure and defined my identity by my failures and defects. This gave me a skewed reality of who I was in God's eyes.

If I'm honest, it also gave me a skewed reality of who I was in my own eyes. I believed I was in a pit of my own making that I could not climb out of, but the truth was I didn't need to climb out by myself. God was reaching in, ready to pull me out and to set me on firm ground with an identity as one he dearly loves.

God calls us to measure our identity by who he is calling us to be. We are sinners saved by grace. All of our troubles are defined by the apostle Paul as "momentary" and "light."[6] What we have now is not what we will have in eternity. We must examine if we are thinking about our identity in light of this.

We need to define our identities not by our momentary, light challenges, but by who we are as children of God, image bearers, and new creations. Those definitions create empowerment and healing.

CHAPTER 10

INTIMACY

*He will tend his flock like a shepherd; he will
gather the lambs in his arms; he will carry them
in his bosom, and gently lead those that are with
young.*

—Isaiah 40:11 ESV

"Intimacy is the fifth spoke in the wheel of the Seven Core
Issues in adoption and permanency. ... Intimacy involves risk,
vulnerability and the belief that the self is valuable and worthy
of love. ... Our primary motivation is to belong, to feel
connected and to learn how to get our emotional needs met
through meaningful, intimate relationships."[1]

When adoptees struggle with identity and confidence in
where they belong, they often have trouble with intimacy.
Negative feelings about themselves and insecurity about their
placement in the family can cause adoptees to lack trust and to
be unwilling to take the risks of vulnerability that are
necessary for intimacy.

I struggled with intimacy in the Haney family but found it
when I had a husband and biological children of my own.

In my teens, the difficulties in my relationship with my
mother amplified after the announcement that my brother
John and I were half-siblings. As I observed the close
relationship some of my friends shared with their mothers, I

longed to be close to mine. That was not to be. We were vastly different people with very different personalities.

That is not to say that we did not love each other. I loved and respected her and learned much from her. It was written about her that "she was known for her hospitality and her graciousness to friends and strangers alike. Her life was a mission field and her confidence in God's faithfulness remains her testimony and legacy to the church."[2]

My mother remained active in her church until well into her eighties. Only when she moved out of her home to live at Quarryville Presbyterian Retirement Community in Lancaster, Pennsylvania, did her Sunday hospitality come to an end. Even at the retirement home, she remained active in Bible studies and correspondence with those who needed encouragement.

She was a relentless encourager to my brother John. To her dying day she prayed for, wrote, called, and encouraged him. She was a true prayer warrior who prayed for each of her children and her nine grandchildren every day. She wrote endless letters to all of us, even sending "pin money" to her grandchildren in college from time to time.

But she was emotionally distant and I felt that disconnect greatly. Her strict upbringing caused her to be legalistic in how she saw things. She ran a very tight ship at home. She had high standards for me and made demands I was not capable of meeting, especially when it came to my brother John. My father continually encouraged me to keep loving her and that, one day, things would change. That did not happen.

One day, in high school, I was called to the front office and told that I had been requested to go home because my mother needed me. I hurried home, thinking something terrible had happened.

I found her calmly cleaning. My journal lay open on the dining room table. Confused, I wondered what the urgency was. Was I in trouble? Had something happened?

Only when she began asking me questions did I make the connection: My mother had read my journal.

When I realized what she had read, I knew that not only was I in trouble, but I could also implicate my friends if I didn't answer carefully. More than that, I was angry at this violation of my privacy. In fact, I was livid.

So, I chose to lie and then refused to answer anything further.

My mother assured me she had every right to do what she did. She justified it by saying she was trying to learn more about John. And this wasn't a one-time occurrence, either. She had been finding and reading my journals for some time, whether I kept them in the open or hid them.

I ripped every page out of that journal, shredded it to bits, and threw it out. Then I gathered my other journals and threw them in a dumpster on my way back to school.

I did not journal again until I left home. And even after I left home and began journaling again, every book that I completed was thrown away. To this day, I regret that. However, I could not bring myself to risk the vulnerability of someone else reading my private thoughts and longings. My mother never felt that she had done anything wrong.

Intimacy was then, understandably, very hard for me. It wasn't until I married and became a mother that I began to soften my heart toward others and let them in.

My husband John and I started our family much sooner than we had planned. While that was challenging, it marked a turning point for me. For the first time in my life, I had a biological connection that helped fill me. I always wanted children and hoped to have a large family. The idea of having someone who was an integral part of me, who was connected by blood and related in every way, was a desire I had felt strongly from the time I was a young girl. I now belonged to someone, and they belonged to me.

When I was pregnant with our oldest, Lynnette, I confessed to a friend that I was afraid of the pain of labor. Her response as a seasoned mother of five was, "Women do this every day and then go on to do it again. You'll be fine!"

But after thirty-six hours of labor that culminated in three hours of pushing that child out of my body, I wasn't sure I ever wanted to do it again. Ironically, within the year I would do just that—fortunately, our son Michael decided ten hours and just a few pushes were enough to deliver him.

Bringing Lynnette home from the hospital, we were smitten. We strapped her in between us on the front bench seat of our Chevy Nova—completely legal in the early eighties. We kept looking from her sweet face to each other, amazed at her perfection and the fact that she came from us.

"She's so beautiful," I said. "We'll have to fight the boys off," John chuckled. "How did we get such a pretty baby?" She's so beautiful." "She looks just like you." And on and on. We were in love.

Even as we celebrated, I was concerned about my own mental health and that of my brother John—and what that could mean for my children. We had finally found a medication that was working for depression, only to be told it was best if I discontinued it during pregnancy. And by this time, my brother John was in and out of rehab for alcohol and drug addiction. I wondered if there was a genetic issue about which I should be concerned.

It would be decades before I met Hazel, but I thought of my then-undiscovered birth mother often as I fed and cared for Lynnette. I wished I could let her know she was a grandma. At the same time, I worried about what genetic risks might even then be working through my child's system.

My mother was extremely helpful, as my parents lived close by. We saw them often, either at our house or theirs. Most Sundays, we went to their home after church and were fed and cared for while Lynnette got lots of attention. I loved this little girl with all my heart and had all kinds of big dreams for her.

With Michael's arrival, we had our hands full. As a one-year-old, Lynnette did not take kindly to her baby brother coming so soon and was up to all sorts of mischief when my back was turned. I could relate to how my mother must have felt with two babies. And we all watched to see if Lynnette would start to bang her head against the wall like I had.

Thankfully, she did not. She found other ways to demand attention, though. Like me, she grew out of them as Michael grew older and did not demand quite as much one-on-one time.

Six months after Michael's birth, my parents moved back to Philadelphia due to my father's poor health. My depression began to spiral downward again. Fortunately, we had a strong support system in place through our church. Many pitched in to help us get through the tough times. I went back on medication and things were looking better. We were able to buy a little townhouse with a backyard for the kids to play in. We loved our little family. The kids became best friends as they grew.

I kept telling myself I should be happy. But that happiness was elusive ... just out of reach. The depression became darkness again.

One trigger for this was my brother John's disappearance. While I don't remember how long it took for us to find out where he was, we eventually learned that he was panhandling at Penn Station in New York City. I was beside myself with worry and anxiety.

It was at this point that my husband said, "Enough!"

I was spending too much time worrying about John and assisting my parents in navigating the situation to find him some help, to the detriment of our family. And it needed to end. When we put that boundary in place, it was such a relief. It did not stem all the worry or anxiety, but I was able to release that burden more fully to God. With the help of Psalm 91, I claimed refuge for John beneath the shadow of the wings of our Heavenly Father and found some peace.

Intimacy returned to our little family along with that peace. My priorities were back in place. We were better able to function as a family unit.

It took some convincing on my part, but when Lynnette and Michael were almost five and four, we decided to have another baby. That year, we traveled to Iowa to see my husband John's family around Thanksgiving. One of his younger brothers was in a coma and the outcome was not promising, so we went to see him and to encourage the family.

While we were there, John's grandmother asked me when I was expecting. I laughed and told her I wasn't pregnant yet but hoped to be soon. She smiled and said, "You are pregnant."

Both John and I thought that was a weird thing to say and had a good laugh about it. When his brother passed away several weeks later and we returned to Iowa for the funeral, I was able to tell her that she had been right—I was indeed pregnant and due at the end of the following summer. "I could see it in your eyes," was her response.

Little did we know what was ahead of us. In the twenty-sixth week of my pregnancy, I was rushed to the hospital with preeclampsia. My liver and kidneys were beginning to shut down.

When my blood reached a dangerous clotting level, I was transferred to a hospital with a higher level of neonatal intensive care. Our tiny one-pound, eight-ounce baby was born by emergency cesarean section on May 24. We'd originally chosen the name Stephanie, but that seemed way too long for a tiny baby. So, we named her Kayla Grace. Her middle name was after my mother.

She spent the next ninety-three days in the hospital. I was in intermediate care for four days and, after being transferred to a regular room, finally got to see her on the fifth day after giving birth. I remained in the hospital for another week.

Our summer was filled with daily trips to the hospital, which was over an hour away from home. Kayla's progress was mostly upward, but we had several challenging days.

During this time, my father began chemotherapy for his ultimately terminal liver cancer. Our hospital made it possible for him to come and hold Kayla before his treatment began. It was a precious family time.

In August, several weeks before her original due date, our baby girl came home—weighing in at four pounds, four ounces. She was on a monitor and had a daily visiting nurse, but she was finally home with her family. We rejoiced in her life and celebrated every milestone with friends and family. She is our miracle!

That September, our church had a special service of thanksgiving. My father was able to baptize Kayla and preached a sermon on God's covenant faithfulness from Genesis 3.

Intimacy is a closeness born of regularity. It is being open and vulnerable with each other, doing life together. Adoptees who struggle with intimacy are almost always really struggling with fear. Deep inside, they are still fearful that rejection could happen again. When that fear remains unspoken and unattended, there is a lack of openness and vulnerability and we lose out on the benefits of intimacy, whether in our marriage, our family unit or our community.

But we need to experience intimacy to move forward in a healthy and meaningful way. Intimacy is recognizing that you are loved and valuable and passing that on to others. What helped me to develop intimacy was having children, growing with them, making mistakes, asking for forgiveness, and doing it all over again the next day. It is the moments experienced over and over again with my family: watching personalities develop, sharing struggles, celebrating victories big and small, and helping each other dream. It is instilling love and value in the next generation.

"The greatest obstacles to discovering deep joy from intimacy with God are the lies we like to believe."[3] Amen! I let three lies define me for the majority of my life. Those lies could not be further from the truth. They came from Satan, who is called the father of lies.[4] By believing those lies of being unwanted, being a failure, and not belonging, I denied God's truth. His truth said that I was wanted—so much so that Jesus would die for me. I wasn't a failure. I was a child of the King and I belonged to the family of God, filled with brothers and sisters and spiritual parents who desired God's best for me.

By believing Satan's lies, I could not enjoy the intimacy of being a part of that family. I felt so alone when I was literally surrounded by an army of those who loved me.

But by seeking God's truth and keeping him at the center of every part of our family life, we can watch his plan for us unfold. It is his plan and his purpose we are striving to reach— for our testimony to his faithfulness and for his glory. We cannot do this when we are sitting in Satan's clutches. And that is what spiritual warfare does: it robs us of intimacy with God.

Just as intimacy within the family grows over time, so does intimacy with God. The more time we spend in his Word, listening to his thoughts and observing his faithfulness throughout time, we will begin to apply the truths we read and hear to our own circumstances. When we choose to ignore prayer, failing to talk to God about our troubles, our concerns, our joys and sorrows, we will find that our lives lack answers and feelings of security.

Just as a lack of communication with a family member or spouse can cause us to feel disconnected, the same thing happens with God. We lose a closeness we had previously enjoyed. We begin to rely on ourselves, we begin to withhold trust, and we entertain resentment when things don't go as we want.

In its simplest form, our spiritual adoption tells us we are loved and have value as a child of God. We earthly parents love and value our children and work to provide everything for them to prosper, and that is what God does for us. The closer we grow to him, the more we see his hand in everything we do.

Familial intimacy and spiritual intimacy go hand in hand. God gives us good and perfect gifts[5] even when our parents might fail. His greatest gift is his love for us, which he showed us by sending his Son to die to save us.[6] When we get to know our heavenly Father, we will experience the vastness of his love for us.[7]

CHAPTER 11

MASTERY AND CONTROL

*The boundary lines have fallen for me in
pleasant places. Indeed, I have a beautiful
inheritance. ... You reveal the path of life to me;
in your presence is abundant joy; at
your right hand are eternal pleasures.*
                                   —Psalm 16:6, 11 CSB

Mastery and control are defined in *Seven Core Issues in Adoption and Permanency* as "proficiency, command or grasp of a subject, skill or knowledge base. It includes mastery over one's life circumstances, which is connected to self-awareness. Control is the power to influence or direct people's behaviors or the course of events. The loss of control over a person's early life journey diminishes their power to direct their future life course."[1]

This last core issue, the dual problem of mastery and control, is one of the hardest for me to write about. But I'm choosing to write about it, because the event that led me to confront it was one of the most pivotal points in my life. It's a season I go back to in my mind, time and again, to recall the wisdom and lessons I learned during this particularly vulnerable period.

In 1994, we had settled into the routine of family life. I was enjoying being a mother to three children and, aside from a part-time job, was able to be home with them most of the time.

The two older kids were in school and Kayla was at home with me. Now four years old, she was growing and making her milestones. It seemed as if we could put the anxiety over her premature birth, and its long aftermath, behind us. It was a peaceful time between my mother and me. I barely even thought about my adoption.

And then I sustained an injury to my back while lifting a box of groceries. That threw everything back into chaos. I could barely move, was unable to stand up straight, and was literally crawling from bed to couch to bathroom and back again. I was prescribed pain medication and muscle relaxers and told to stay on bed rest for six weeks. My mother came down from Pennsylvania to help, and our church and neighbors pitched in as well.

Depression set in with a ferociousness I had never before experienced. If you have experienced issues with chronic pain, you know the helplessness I was feeling. Physical pain can cause mental and emotional pain. Inactivity brought up my thoughts and insecurities about my adoption and the lies I still believed about myself at this point in time.

The more time I had on my hands, the darker my thoughts became.

While my back did improve over those six weeks, giving me more mobility, I was still experiencing pain and numbness down the right side of my leg. The nerve damage was causing me to limp, which resulted in other problems due to my uneven gait.

Visits to my doctor, a neurologist, and a physical therapist were able to relieve some of the pain, but there were frequent times when the pain was so intense, it caused me to gasp involuntarily—I could not even move.

Little by little, I felt better physically and could reduce the amount of pain meds, just taking them as needed. However, mentally, I was in a very low place.

The holidays came and went. Shortly after, I visited my doctor to see about increasing my dosage for the depression I was experiencing.

When he asked me if I wanted to harm myself, I burst into tears and told him, "Yes."

This was the first time I admitted out loud to a medical professional that I needed help, that I knew how I would end my life. After a lengthy talk, we agreed that I would try an increase in medication, seek counseling from my pastor, and have regular check-ins.

Of course, my husband was made aware, along with my neighbor and good friend Linda. If anything were to change, I was being monitored and closely watched.

After several counseling sessions with my pastor, he asked if I would be amenable to seeing a professional counselor. He mentioned a Christian counselor, Pat, who had experience counseling several of the issues that I was struggling with, including issues surrounding adoption. Pat was easy to talk with and had worked with many unwed mothers who had chosen adoption, giving me a new perspective on the many reasons why a baby would be relinquished. She assured me that these choices were never made without a lot of thought and love for the child. While her guidance was extremely helpful to my understanding of adoption, I continued to deteriorate physically and mentally due to the pain I was experiencing.

It reached the point where my team of caregivers determined that inpatient therapy would be more helpful. I was admitted to a program called New Life at a local hospital. It was an eye-opener.

I remember feeling angry and stupid. Filled with shame and regret for having spoken up, I berated myself. I thought, "Now I am just like my brother." He had been in and out of institutions just like this one and here I was locked behind doors and under observation, like a fish in a fishbowl. It was humiliating to watch them go through my belongings and remove everything that I might be able to use for harm. I felt like a small child. I had lost all control over my life at that moment.

I made it very clear that no one was to know I was here—not friends, not family, not my parents.

I was given a choice: Do the work and feel better or go home. I knew going home was not an option. So, I settled in for the two required inpatient weeks and did the work. The days were filled with group counseling, individual counseling, and physical exercise, which I could only watch as my pain was still an issue. We also had art and music therapy and homework assignments for the next day. There was very little down time.

I quickly learned everything about the dozen other people who were my daily companions, and they learned everything about me. Nothing stayed hidden. Everything was fair game in conversations toward healing.

The issues that came to focus for me were my adoption, my relationship with my mother, my brother John, and my father's cancer. I was surprised by the last one, but I realized how much I relied on his love and for his counsel.

We methodically worked through each of those issues. I realized several things about myself, but mostly I unbottled lots and lots of anger. Many of the things that came out of my mouth surprised me and I filled pages and pages in a notebook. It was a cleansing experience; it was something I needed to do to heal from the inside out.

Following two more weeks of daily outpatient therapy, I was able to return to my own counselor for treatment after being discharged. I was changed. Emptying out all the poison left me feeling so much lighter. Now I needed to find ways to begin to fill that emptiness with positive things.

During my time in the hospital, I learned that, even though I was in the psych ward, I still had access to several skilled doctors who could help me with my physical challenges. One of those happened to be a neurologist, who was asked to provide a consultation on my back pain and limp.

He was a gift from God. He told me that, if I'd been in my eighties, he wouldn't be able to do anything—but since I was only thirty-three, he thought surgery might correct some, if not all, of the problem. About a month after my discharge, I underwent back surgery and felt relief for the next ten years, even though some of the nerve damage was permanent.

I was also treated for a sleep disorder and for my migraines. Although I still wrestle with both to this day, I have found some relief.

The biggest thing I gained was information and answers. Knowledge is power, and I began to take back parts of my life over which, up to this point, I had little control. Now I had the knowledge to find solutions that could stop things from spiraling out of control again. Journaling, music, and art all became outlets to express my thoughts and release mental and emotional pain. Creating things helped me to find joy that spilled over into other parts of my life.

Here are three truths I learned from this time that are helpful for the rest of my life:

1. Grief and pain go hand in hand. The pain of grief can cause physical pain. Many of the things that I sought counseling for—my adoption, my relationship with my mother, my inability to do anything for my brother John, and mistakes I made in my teens—were all things I grieved. From that grief came physical pain, which manifested itself in my body in ways that I already physically suffered: migraines, insomnia, back pain, nerve pain, anxiety, and depression.

2. My story mattered—all of it. The lies I believed were just that: lies. It was Satan's way of keeping me weak. Yet God was my strength in that weakness. His truth was that I was beloved and an heir of righteousness despite my struggles with sin, because of Jesus. His truth comforted the little girl who had ugliness interjected into her adoption story. His truth took that burden of responsibility from the teenager who had no way to help a sibling with addiction and mental illness. And God collected my tears and counted each one,[2] loving me with an everlasting love. "His truth is strong enough to absorb the lies that we are tempted to buy when we are in pain."[3]

3. Spiritual resilience is key. When I felt that I had reached the end of my endurance, that I could not continue in the mental and emotional pain, God said, "No," loudly and clearly. This was not the end. When he says no, he provides a way out. The way out is truth, and truth is found in his Word. If we want spiritual resilience that enables us to return from "the pit,"[4] we need to abide in his Word. When we "sit in God's presence, ... [our] doubts find their resolution in the certainty that God is not only faithful, but also impossibly, immutably good."[5]

Spending time in God's Word instead of time in my own head changed how I thought about everything. Gratitude and thankfulness for his faithfulness in my life became paramount to driving away the fear and doubt that tried to reside in my mind.

My thoughts about my adoption slowly changed from negative and ugly to positive and joy-filled. As a result, I became a more positive person, both in my inner thoughts and in the way I treated myself and those around me. Spiritual resilience brought light into my life.

I am very thankful to God for the people and programs that I experienced at this point in my life. In surrender to him is where I see his control over my life. His ongoing promises sustain us in our darkest hours.

Several Bible verses that I committed to memory now replaced the thoughts of being unwanted and a failure. "I will never leave you or abandon you"[6] and "his mercies never end; they are new every morning; great is your faithfulness!"[7] became words of comfort that drove out fear and inadequacy.

I recently came across some helpful encouragement while reading *Beyond Our Control* by Lauren and Michael McAfee. They express the lessons I learned about mastery and control in a way that resonates with my soul:

> *Life gets messy. Things feel hard. We are made to deal with our own blind spots; we are made to wrestle with emotions we don't want to feel; we are made to fall flat on our face a thousand times, having nowhere to look but up. ... If we choose to look up, we'll find comfort. We'll find healing. We'll find hope. ... Intimacy with Jesus is the goal. It is what allows us to see that the greatest joy we'll ever know is being totally out of control. For it is in that place of complete surrender that his power surges strong.[8]*

Many adoptees feel their life story is completely out of their control simply because it began with loss and contains questions they don't know the answers to. But when we know God, experience his character, and immerse ourselves in his Word to us, we will find that the one who controls all things has our best interest at heart. His love for us will become increasingly evident when we lean into all he says about us and the plan he has for us. The hard things are temporary. He is the one who gives us hope and a future.[9]

Spiritual adoption models for us how to relinquish control. It takes us from the control of sin, which the Bible calls slavery,[10] to a kingdom of light and joy. As adopted children of God, we are part of that kingdom. Eventually, that kingdom will replace all the pain of what we do not know with the joy of what we do know: that we are loved, that we belong, that we are valued. Until that time, we trust that he will be faithful.

Toward the end of her life, my mother and I would often end our phone calls with the simple phrase, "Keep looking up!" We look up because that is where we will find Jesus. It was our way of pointing each other to the one who meets our every need, to the one we trust in.

Trust is an act of obedience; it doesn't always come easily. Trust is faith in the assurance of things hoped for, the conviction of things not seen.[11]

As I've shared my story of how I experienced the core issues often seen in adoption, I hope you've seen that it has always been my spiritual adoption that has provided the answers to those issues.

For every lie, there is a truth that can set us free if we will only accept it. I accepted the truth of the gospel at a very young age and, thanks to my parents' diligence in teaching me when I was young, those truths were never far from me—even when I strayed.

I may have taken some detours and even had to do some U-turns, but God's truth was never far from me. He gently called me back every time I stepped too far from the path of grace.

It is never too late to begin the journey of spiritual adoption. In Part 3, we will dive deeper into the truth about adoption, both physical adoption and spiritual adoption.

PART 3
TRUTH THAT TRANSFORMS
AND BRINGS HOPE

As children adopted by God,
you and I have a story that people are
desperate to hear.
It's the gospel story.
It's a story that gives hope.
It's the story of redemption.

CHAPTER 12

TELLING OURSELVES THE TRUTH

*And you will know the truth, and the truth will
set you free.*

—John 8:32 ESV

This is the best part of the story: the truths that give us
hope.

The core issues we just explored are all typical responses
found in the lived experience of many adoptees. But no
adoptee, including me, needs to remain stuck in any of the
core issues.

Our culture tends to get stuck there, though, developing a
victim mentality of hurt and pain. There is a better way to look
at adoption. In fact, spiritual adoption is the original plan of
adoption and is available not only to adoptees, but to anyone
who comes to Jesus in faith.

Before time began, God the Father made a way for us to be
adopted as his sons and daughters. Spiritual adoption is the
answer to the longings and cries of our heart, not only for the
adoptee and other members of the adoption triad, but for all
who will seek Jesus.

Spiritual adoption replaces:
- Loss with gain
- Rejection with acceptance
- Shame and guilt with grace

- Grief with hope

Spiritual adoption gives us:
- A new identity in Christ
- Intimacy with Abba, our heavenly Father
- Access to the One who holds all things in control

As Jesus said, "you will know the truth, and the truth will set you free."[1] The truth that sets us free is the truth of the gospel. It is a free gift available to all who seek him.

What Is the Truth of the Gospel?

The Bible, the Word of God, tells us that we are all sinners and deserve death. Sin is rebellion against God. When the first man, Adam, disobeyed God in the Garden of Eden, he brought sin into the world and to all people. "Therefore, just as sin entered the world through one man, and death through sin, in this way death spread to all people, because all sinned."[2]

God sent his Son, Jesus, to take our punishment and to die in our place on the cross. "For God so loved the world, that he gave his only Son, that whoever believes in him should not perish but have eternal life."[3]

This is the gift of salvation that comes from God. We cannot earn it. The only way to receive this gift is through Jesus' redemptive work on our behalf. No one receives this gift without believing this truth. Jesus says, "I am the way, and the truth, and the life. No one comes to the Father except through me."[4]

When we receive this truth and believe it by faith, we are called the sons and daughters of God. "But to all who did receive him, who believed in his name, he gave the right to become children of God."[5]

God sent Jesus to redeem us, "so that we might receive adoption as sons."[6]

As adopted sons and daughters, our lives are transformed. We have new truths. No longer are we held prisoners by the lies that Satan wants us to believe. God answers those lies with truth.

What Truth Answers the Lies I Believed?

Thoughtless words can hurt. They hurt as a child, and they hurt as an adult. Once words escape from our lips they are gone; the damage is done. If words have hurt you like they have me, remember that God's word tells us that he delights in us. "He will rejoice over you with gladness; he will quiet you by his love, he will exult over you with loud singing."[7]

What truth can answer the lies that Satan used to confuse my mind as a young girl? What does God say to any child who feels abandoned and unwanted?

- "I will never leave you or abandon you."[8]
- "See what kind of love the Father has given to us, that we should be called children of God; and so we are."[9]
- "For he chose us in him, before the foundation of the world, to be holy and blameless in love before him."[10]

What truth can answer the lies that consumed me as a teen and young adult? How does God answer our repeated perceived failure and deep depression?

- "I have called you by name, you are mine."[11]

- "When you pass through the waters, I will be with you, and the rivers will not overwhelm you. When you walk through the fire, you will not be scorched, and the flame will not burn you."[12]
- "The one who lives under the protection of the Most High dwells in the shadow of the Almighty. ... He will cover you with his feathers; you will take refuge under his wings."[13]

We do not suffer in isolation. Satan wants us to think we are alone, but the truth is that God is in the pain with us. He took on human flesh and suffered as we do. He knows. He protects us. He carries us. He promises rescue.

What about the lie that caught me unaware as an adult? How does God respond to the doubt of my status as a member of my adopted family?

- "Now if we are children, then we are heirs—heirs of God and co-heirs with Christ."[14]
- "You are no longer a slave, but a son, and if a son, then an heir through God."[15]
- "So, then, you are no longer foreigners and strangers, but fellow citizens with the saints, and members of God's household."[16]

We are family. The blood of Jesus redeems us. That is the only bloodline that truly matters. His blood was willingly shed for you and for me on the cross. Because of it, we can be members of his family and heirs of God, co-heirs with Christ.

Even though I knew each of the lies I believed were false, they still became embedded as truth in my mind, causing great spiritual harm for many years. While we live on this earth, we must deal with our fallen, sinful nature. It causes us to return to the lies, even when we know the real truth.

Each of these lies were caused by careless words from others. How often have our words cut someone down when we should be striving to build one another up? Words are able to give life and to snatch it away. This is the spiritual warfare that Satan wages on us. The Bible clearly tells us that this is who we are struggling against in Ephesians 6:12. It tells us that we are not struggling against flesh and blood but against the powers of darkness, against spiritual forces of evil. This battle goes on in our minds. It is subtle. It is powerful. It is dangerous.

This is why a strong spiritual foundation is crucial, and why spiritual formation is necessary to continue to grow as God's children. I do not know where I would be today without the spiritual foundation that I was given. I am thankful for the teaching and the spiritual disciplines that my parents instilled in me during my childhood and for the reinforcement from church and school throughout my formative years.

It's never too late to begin to build a strong foundation. When Jesus calls us to follow Him, he doesn't leave us to figure it out ourselves. Jesus promised to give the Holy Spirit to believers after his time was completed on earth. The Holy Spirit is referred to in the Bible as the Comforter and the Counselor, among other titles. The Holy Spirit lives in us and directs us to his Word and his people: the church.[17]

I am thankful for the many people who spoke truth into my life during troubled times, who continue to speak truth. I was just an ordinary girl, but God had a wonderful plan for me. He knew who I needed to guide me to the truth.

God's truth keeps us from getting stuck in a victim mentality. It allows us to move forward, into the community and the new life that he provides for us. Far too often, we let the past dictate the future. We make decisions based on things that no longer have relevance for today. We allow past grievances to define our present reality. We need to step forward with courage. Leaving the past behind is biblical. The apostle Paul urges us to push forward with endurance: "let us lay aside every hindrance and the sin that so easily ensnares us. Let us run with endurance the race that lies before us."[18]

My physical adoption story was not perfect for any of those involved, but it was good. Extraordinary, to be specific. I was loved. I had a family. I was pointed to Christ.

But my physical adoption pales in comparison to my spiritual adoption and the joy of being called a daughter of God the Father himself. A daughter that he rejoices over. A daughter that he calls, "Beloved."

Paul David Tripp writes to adoptive parents, "Adoption will take you beyond the borders of your natural wisdom, love, patience, and strength...In your weakness you are the moment by moment recipient of the powerful grace of a loving Lord who understands exactly what you are going through."[19]

When we believe and hold onto these truths, we do not have to be victims of painful adoption circumstances that are often outside of our control. The gospel gives us the truth we need to see the bigger picture of our life. The gospel shows us unconditional love. The gospel gives us hope for the future.

Questions for Thought

- What lies do you believe about your identity?
- How does God's truth respond to those lies?
- What is the first step you need to take to claim God's truth and use it to drive away the power of the lies?

I would encourage you to start with the Scriptures outlined in this and other chapters. Dig into the Word of God. The book of John is a good place to start. Embrace the truth as you read.

CHAPTER 13

THE TRUTH ABOUT ADOPTION

See what great love the Father has lavished on
us, that we should be called children of God!
And that is what we are!

—*1 John 3:1 NIV*

Why does my story matter? For that matter, why does
anyone's story matter?

Our stories matter because God wrote them. "All my days
were written in your book and planned before a single one of
them began."[1]

No one knows us more intimately than God. No one
understands us more personally than God. No one loves us
more abundantly than God.

God is not a great puppet master in the sky, as some would
like to believe. God knows we are broken and sinful people. He
grieves over sin in the world and its effect on our lives. He
shares in our griefs and sorrows and rejoices with us in our
celebrations. We are never alone. But that doesn't mean that
life is easy.

Earthly adoption is hard. It is hard for the birth mother.
There are many different scenarios for why a woman may find
herself in this hard place. She may be a teenager and is too
young to manage a child. She may be a single mom who
struggles to get by and has no way to provide for a baby. She
could have mental health issues or an addiction that controls

her. It would be wrong to not also acknowledge the birth father, his role in the decision-making process, and the potential loss he may feel.

It is hard for the adoptive parents, many of whom have had to deal with their own losses—infertility or the loss of a child—and who also have many questions as they parent a child who struggles with identity and belonging.

And, of course, it is hard for the adoptee. I've explored many of the issues an adoptee may struggle with throughout this book, drawing from my own experiences.

Adoption is hard because we live in a fallen world. Sin entered the world in the beginning. We first read about it in Genesis 3. God made a way to redeem sinners, you and me, through spiritual adoption by giving his Son Jesus to pay the price for sin. God redeems the hard things. He writes our stories to show his glory.

"Do not remember the past events; pay no attention to things of old. Look, I am about to do something new; even now it is coming. Do you not see it? Indeed, I will make a way in the wilderness, rivers in the desert."[2]

God is making all things new.[3] He is making us into new creations.[4] He has promised us a new heaven and a new earth.[5] He has promised to return.[6] He gives us hope for tomorrow and hope for the future.[7]

For every difficult part of my story, there is a hidden treasure. The same is true for you. Unfortunately, that truth is becoming increasingly countercultural.

What Is the Cultural View of Adoption?

I am not an expert by any means, but as I researched for this book, I learned more about the current culture of adoption. I read several memoirs about adoption experiences, both by Christians and non-Christians. I continued to look for solutions to the issues that I experienced in my own adoption story.

Originally, when the book *Seven Core Issues in Adoption and Permanency* was published, there were seven issues identified. The modern model, as put forth by Marie Dolfi, now has twelve issues, adding: abandonment, fitting in, entitlement, loyalty, and claiming. These twelve are now called the core issues of adoption. On her website, Dolfi explains:

> *If you unpack the core issues with a trauma-focused lens, it helps to understand the depths of the adoption triad member's struggles. The extensive stress of adoption trauma experiences changes an individual's view of themselves and their world. Long after relinquishment and adoption traumatic events have passed an individual's brain and body react as if their traumatic experiences are happening in the present. New encounters are viewed through the lens of traumatic experience.[3]*

Dolfi also theorizes that loss is not the only source of every core issue an adoptee faces, but that contributing factors also include how adoption triad members have been treated by other individuals, society, adoption professionals, and adoption laws and practices.[4]

I can relate to the data on the original seven issues as outlined in my story. However, as I researched for this book, I found myself growing alarmed at some of the viewpoints held by today's adoption culture. What I found particularly alarming is that many people seem to be stuck in the mindset of being a victim of traumatic loss. They allow it to write their story. People seem angry, vulnerable and afraid. I experienced much of this as well, until I allowed the Holy Spirit to work in me to find joy in my life—living a life of victory instead of living as a victim.

Christians gladly embrace our spiritual adoption as a picture of the truth of adoption. We are lost sinners, abandoned to death without the solution God has prepared for us through Jesus and faith in Him. "Loss" and "abandoned" are key words in both physical and spiritual adoption. However, the solution to the loss and abandonment—Jesus—is only seen in the spiritual model. While Jesus can bring redemption to physical adoption, and physical adoption can also bring a lot of good, our current culture refuses to believe that physical adoption can be anything but traumatic loss. I am not saying that there is no traumatic loss. I am only emphasizing that in today's world everything about adoption is coated in traumatic loss. The view today is, "No, no, no, adoption is the wrong solution for any part of the triad," leaving us with trauma on all fronts.

Non-Christians do not accept spiritual adoption as a point of reference because they don't understand it. Their hearts are hardened. They are not open to the idea that God is sovereign and in control of all things. Without that truth, it's not surprising that the cultural view of adoption has become increasingly negative. I have been exposed to the U.S. foster care system and the international orphan crisis and have seen up close what adoption looks like on both fronts. These are broken systems—and the results of that breakdown can often be devastating to the very children and parents they are supposed to serve.

At the same time I was researching for my book, a new book was published: *Adoption Unfiltered: Revelations from Adoptees, Birth Parents, Adoptive Parents, and Allies*, in which three authors take on the topic of adoption through their own stories, along with the stories of over fifty adoption triad members.

It was hailed as a "groundbreaking work, the most important book of our modern adoption generation, and even a dream come true."[5] I was excited to check it out of the library ... until I got it home and began to read it.

On the back cover, I found this review: "*Adoption Unfiltered* offers an unsparing deconstruction of the happy-ever-after conventional wisdom about adoption as it crushes the familiar tropes that portray adopters as saviors, birthparents as selfless, and adoptees as blank slates who need nothing more to flourish than a loving stable home."[6]

"Crushes" was a good word choice. Even the three chapters on the effects of religion in adoption were unrecognizable to me as anything other than bitterness and resentment. It seemed as though the authors were trying hard to not find anything good.

One contributor, identified as a Christian birth mother, says, "Adoption wouldn't exist in a perfect world—the world which God intended in the first place—therefore I don't think adoption, which includes layers of emotion, pain, and grief no matter the outcome, should ever be distorted with such simplicity by saying it was 'God's plan'."[7]

The author then goes on to say, "If adoption is God's plan, then God is an exclusionary deity, picking blessings off vulnerable mothers and redistributing them to more financially able families."[8]

Another contributor, who also identifies as religious, says, "You will never convince me that God's plan was for me and my son to be separated just to build a family."[9]

This thought was echoed on the Instagram account @thearchibaldproject, with this comment by a reader: "This is why adoption is horribly, horribly wrong."

A few adoption triad members did share stories of finding solace in religion and spirituality, but it seemed that the God whom I serve was unrecognizable. The god they wrote about was just that—a "little g" god.

And this bleak view of adoption in our culture is just ramping up, now that *Roe v. Wade* has been overturned.

What Is the Truth About Adoption?

In adoption:

- A mother finds herself pregnant with a child that she cannot or will not care for.
- A child is relinquished, therefore needing a home and a family.
- An adoptive parent or parents come forward to love and care for the child, bringing the child into the family as if they were their own flesh and blood, with all the rights and privileges of being a member of that family.
- Everyone involved in this scenario will have consequences, both good and bad, based on decisions made outside their control.
- These consequences will span the lifetime of each person involved.

The truth is a child in need of love and devotion receives a family who loves and devotes themselves to this child who needs them. And yes, adoptions can go terribly wrong. But that doesn't mean that God can't or won't redeem the story.

We need to acknowledge that there is hurt and pain involved in adoption for all parties. But we need to look to the Savior for healing of that hurt and pain. We do not need to stay in brokenness.

In his book, *Adopted for Life,* Russell Moore titles one of his chapters, "Adopted Is a Past-Tense Verb." In that chapter, he writes that adoption is not an adjective, nor a label for the one who is adopted. Rather, it is an action that has taken place. Moore goes on to say:

> *In the post-Fall world, being part of a family is tough, regardless of the circumstances. Adoption complicates that already complicated reality even further. We need to be aware of the common struggles that come with growing up adopted. Like the event of adoption itself these struggles can, if we have ears to hear and eyes to see, point us to the gospel that saves us.*[10]

We are living in a fallen world and until Jesus returns, we will have trouble. Jesus himself says, "In this world you will have trouble. But take heart! I have overcome the world."[11]

Having trouble and remaining stuck in trouble are two different things. Our secular culture embraces the victim mentality. But Jesus has overcome the victim mentality for us. We are no longer slaves to fear, we are children of God.[12] A child of God does not have to remain in victim mode. Our thinking should follow what we know to be true about what God has done for us and how he views us. This is a good exercise to do when we feel the weight of brokenness. What do we know to be true about God? What Scripture can we find to corroborate that truth? How does that truth make us less of a victim and more of a victor? Write the answers down. Keep the list and expand it every time you begin to return to a victim mentality.

In the constant spiritual warfare Satan wages on us, he will tell you that pain of loss and rejection define who you are, and that you must immerse yourself in that guilt, shame, and grief. Lies are the tools that Satan uses. But God gives us a more powerful tool, his Word as our "sword," and when we wield it, we have the most effective weapon for battle.[13]

Ruth Chou Simons, Christian artist and author, often uses the phrase, "preaching truth to yourself."[14]

Preaching truth to yourself means that you keep renewing your mind[15] by taking "captive every thought to make it obedient to Christ."[16] This means that we remind ourselves daily what we know to be true about who God is, who we are because of Christ, and the truth about his purpose for our life. Take that list you made and put it to use to preach truth to yourself and win the daily battle for your mind.

It is proactive work—changing the narrative that goes on in our mind and being careful about the messages we choose to allow into our thoughts and believe about ourselves. We say "stop" to the whispers from Satan about being unworthy and a failure. We replace those thoughts with Scriptures such as, "I have called you by name, you are mine."[17] To do this, we must read and memorize Scripture so that we can replace Satan's words with God's words in an instant.

Christians don't have all the answers, but we have *the* answer. We are not powerless against Satan's schemes. We are not powerless because we have the truth on our side and can be prepared for the daily battle. We have resources for our most difficult seasons. Our feelings and fears no longer have control when we put our faith and trust in God. Trust is an act of obedience, daily believing that his plan for us is better than anything we could derive on our own.

Adoption affects more than just the adoptee. I've seen that truth play out in my story. But it goes even further than the adoption triad. It continues into the nuclear family, including children and grandchildren. Their story also becomes one of adoption. My children's and grandchildren's stories will always have the same holes as mine.

The Lord gave me a wonderful—and very patient—husband and he blessed us with our three beautiful children. We made almost every parenting mistake in the book, but Lynnette, Michael, and Kayla still turned out to be independent adults who are smarter and better looking than their parents. More importantly, they love and trust Jesus Christ with their very lives.

My biggest concern, aside from their spiritual lives, has always been for their physical and mental health, watching for anything that might signal a problem from my unknown genetics. But, at some point, we must give our fears and worries over to God. We are not slaves to fear, and disaster is not waiting around every corner just because adoption is part of the equation.

How many families meet obstacles and challenges that come as complete surprises? Data would show the number to be astronomical. This is the world we live in.

I have been involved in disability ministry for almost 20 years. I began by volunteering as a teacher at my church. Currently I sit on the Board of Hope Learning Center, a non-profit that works with young adults on the autism spectrum and more recently, began leading a care group for moms of children and young adults with a wide range of disabilities. I see many parallels to adoption. Loss, rejection, guilt and shame, grief, identity, and mastery and control are not issues solely relegated to the adoption triad. Every family I know that lives with disability experiences most of these daily. They also deal with many unknowns and have questions that will not be answered this side of eternity.

Jesus addresses this in John 9. When he and his disciples passed by a man who was born blind, his disciples asked whether the man or his parents sinned to cause his condition. "'Neither this man nor his parents sinned,' Jesus answered.

'This came about so that God's works might be displayed in him.'"[18]

God is at work through disability, through adoption, and through our brokenness, so that his works might be displayed through us. In faith, we move forward through the unknown, knowing that we have a faithful God who knows everything, who walks beside us.[19]

We can leave the seven or twelve or however many the number of issues there are behind because we go forward with contentment in the story God has written for us. We move forward with joy, knowing that God is redeeming our lives. Instead of looking back we look ahead with hope – knowing and embracing the truth about the God who created us and loves us.

After finding Hazel, I decided to search for relatives on my birth father's side on Ancestry.com. I spit into the test tube and mailed my sample off, waiting eagerly to see what I might find. While the search led me to several more family members on Hazel's side, I only ever received one response from what I assume was my birth father's side of the equation.

One afternoon, an email informed me that I had another match. When I went to the website to read the message, I saw it was from someone identified as a potential first cousin.

It read, "This ought to be good! Who are you?"

A little taken aback by the tone of the comment, I hesitated before responding. Eventually I wrote, "I was adopted in 1962 and am interested in finding information about people I may be related to. I have found much of my birth mother's family and am hoping to find something about my birth father. Would this fit anyone from your family?"

There was silence. Nothing was ever written back, and I did not pursue it.

I wasn't afraid to pursue it. I was just done pursuing. I had enough. I had the best earthly father a girl could ask for and I had a heavenly Father that graciously met my every need. What more could I need or want?

The search was over. I was content with what I had already found.

I know God wrote all of my story and that one day I will have whatever answers he deems necessary. I move forward with joy because I know I am a child of God, saved by grace and redeemed by the blood of Jesus. And I look forward in hope to an eternity where there will be no more searching or questioning, no more hurt and pain. I am confident in the identity God has given me through spiritual adoption and through my physical adoption into the Haney family.

Questions for Thought

- What narratives about adoption have informed your perspective on it? Are you reconsidering any of them?
- What core issues of adoption have you personally struggled with?
- Does your faith make a difference in how you respond to those struggles?

CHAPTER 14

FINDING HOPE IN THE TRUTH

*And we know that for those who love God all
things work together for good, for those who
are called according to his purpose.*
—Romans 8:28 ESV

Writing out one's story with honesty about the hard times—the sins, failures and pain—is not an easy task. Looking back on my life, I see the hand of God at work in all seasons, the good and the bad. Writing about it is an exercise that is at times therapeutic, often terrifying, and frequently exciting. Ralph Waldo Emerson once said, "All I have seen teaches me to trust the Creator for all I have not seen."[1] I heartily agree.

Many times, I have looked back at what I have written and said to myself, "Look what God has done!" Without the hard times, I would not be refined into the person God wants me to be. I think of the process of refining metal. Metal must go through the intense heat of a white hot fire and then be molded with sharp pounds of the hammer to become a blade or be curved into a horseshoe the exact size of a horse's hoof. Pain and struggles in our lives are part of a refining process that teaches us to look to the one who created us, rather than relying on ourselves.

That imagery came to mind as I finished the final draft of this book. I felt as though I had been refined by recalling the dark times. I now saw them with a fresh perspective of how God had carried me through to the other side.

Little did I know that, as I dug deep and wrote my story, God was preparing me for another dark time that I did not want and was not expecting. About a month after typing the last words of this manuscript, a suspicious mass was found on an x-ray of my chest. After many tests and scans, I was diagnosed with lung cancer.

Not only was I diagnosed with a dreaded disease, I also learned that it was caused by a genetic mutation. My unknown genetic makeup had come out of hiding. As the doctors asked me questions about my family history, I had few answers, even with the little bit I did know thanks to Hazel's sister.

This diagnosis was a shock. But, having so recently seen the faithfulness of God throughout my story, I did not fear the outcome, nor did I fear the future. I knew I was wrapped in the arms of my heavenly Father who had always provided well for me, and I knew he would again.

I was anxious about pain and procedures and undergoing surgery that would remove a portion of my lung. I was frustrated that, after years of working on my health and feeling well, I was about to enter another period of life where I would most likely feel really bad.

But God, in his mercy, went before us and prepared excellent doctors and a top-notch cancer center that would meet our needs. All of my cancer was removed through surgery and chemo and radiation were deemed not necessary.

It was a miraculous outcome that far exceeded the expectations set in the initial diagnosis. We again saw God's faithfulness and his care of us through the prayers of many people.

I am in an aggressive follow-up program for the next five years to make sure the cancer doesn't return and to monitor the genetic issue that was found. But cancer is just another chapter in my story. It does not define me.

Neither does my physical adoption define who I am. God defines me through sanctification—the act of purifying and making one holy. God used adoption to place me exactly where he wanted me to be, with all the experiences I have had and the people who he brought into my life. God chose this path for me.

My husband explained it to a friend this way: "I'm so grateful that Hazel chose adoption. Without adoption, we wouldn't have us or our family." While God can certainly do anything in any way, John is referring to the path that led me to Covenant College and eventually to him. I was also reminded that one of Hazel's wishes for her Baby Girl was that I had the opportunity to go to college—an opportunity she knew she could not give me. But God knew what was waiting for me at Covenant, and he knew it would be for my good.

We recently had the opportunity to attend John's fortieth class reunion at Covenant College. During our return to Lookout Mountain, we reminisced about people who had been important to us during our time together. We visited places that were meaningful to us. We drove by our first home. We spent some time watching hang glider pilots jump off the mountain, which had been a common afternoon date for us back in the day.

It's a tradition at Covenant to climb to the top of the tower at school and sign your name on the inside wall. Neither of us had taken advantage of it while we attended, so we did it together then.

God's plan for my life included my adoption story and even the broken parts in my life, Hazel's life, and my parents' lives. He knew how each of those stories could and would be used to glorify Him. Instead of just seeing traumatic loss and lifelong struggle, I now see the blessing it was to be placed in the

Haney family. God blessed me with a family who loved and cared for me, blessed my family with a daughter and sister who loved and supported them, and blessed Hazel with the gift of seeing everything that he did from the impossible situation she found herself in as a young woman. Her simple wish for her Baby Girl was that she would grow up in a two-parent family and go to college. What her daughter received was so much more.

I started this chapter with Romans 8:28. It's often used as a "feel good" verse when one is in a hard place. "Things will be good because God is good," is what people want to hear and believe. But our vision of what's good is often not what God sees as good. And many times, we do not understand why or how the end result of our circumstances or struggles could possibly be construed as something good.

I see that in many places in my story. The burdens of depression, suicidal thoughts, chronic pain, memories from assault, the loss of people on which I relied, relationship struggles, and other difficulties I experienced are not what I call "good."

They were hard, devastating at times, especially when there seemed no end in sight. But when I look back, I see how God worked them out for my good. Not in a linear way. Rather, as my life's timeline develops, I see the good weaving in and over and around to mold me into the woman he is calling me to be.

Sometimes we have to look hard for the good. In some cases, we may have to wait for and trust in the hope of heaven to see what good God intended for us. But if we trust that good is there, and believe God's promises for the interim, we will be able to testify to his goodness. We will know that good is weaving through our lives for his glory.

And one day all will be made new—when all sin and sorrow will be wiped away. When bad memories will be no more.

When Satan is destroyed and the spiritual battle is won. This is the ultimate good God has in store for his children.

If you are struggling with finding good in your story, whether it is an adoption story or not, I want to encourage you to stop struggling for just a moment. Take a minute to remind yourself that God is good. There is nothing he cannot do. Your struggle may feel horribly dark right now, with no way out. But think, for just a minute, of his promise that there is treasure in the darkness and riches in secret places.

"I will give you the treasures of darkness and riches from secret places, so that you may know that I am the Lord. I am the God of Israel who calls you by your name."[2]

The treasure lies in the fact that God is there with you. You do not need to fear. You are not alone. God promises he will hold you with his righteous right hand.[3]

The riches in the secret places are that God is caring for you. He knows every single day of your life[4] and every single hair on your head.[5]

He will provide for you. The apostle Peter tells us we should be "casting all your cares on him, because he cares about you."[6]

And he will sustain you. "I am he who will sustain you. I have made you and I will carry you; I will sustain you and I will rescue you."[7]

If your struggle *is* your adoption story and you have more questions than answers, hold on. Remember, if you believe in Jesus Christ as your Savior, you are a child of God. Your heritage is written in the Book of Life, and one day all will be made right. It will all be redeemed and it will all be good.

When we view our struggles through a biblical lens, we will always see that God is sovereign. He is wise and loving. The last part of Romans 8:28 uses the phrase "according to his purpose." God's purpose is sovereign because God is sovereign. He knows all the details. He knows the before and after, the now and not yet. We trust that he is good and leave the rest to him, knowing one day, our questions will be answered.

And for now, he knows the answers. And that is enough.

For over a decade, I spoke at women's retreats and taught several classes on the classic book, *The Pilgrim's Progress by John Bunyan* through Bible studies, Sunday school and a middle school Bible class. During these presentations, I shared some stories from my spiritual journey that illustrated many of the points made in the book.

One of the stories that I shared frequently was a climb that I did with my brothers David and John as teenagers up Mount Katahdin in Baxter State Park, Maine. It is the highest mountain in Maine and the northeast terminus for the Appalachian Trail. The terrain is rough and, depending on the trails you take, reaching the summit can take eight to twelve hours. We had never done anything like this.

My father, who had climbed it with youth groups when he pastored the church in Bangor, wanted us to experience this climb. He put the trip together with a longtime family friend who lived nearby in Presque Isle, Maine. He had also climbed it many times and acted as our guide.

It was April in Maine, which is very chilly. We braced ourselves for a vigorous climb, especially after being told we'd have to take a challenging trail and keep up our speed to reach the summit and return all the way down before dark.

The first three-and-a-half miles were fairly easy hiking. Then, we moved onto the next phase, taking Cathedral Trail. I have since read Cathedral Trail described as climbing over huge Jenga blocks. It is an apt description. We were no longer hiking a trail—we were climbing a mountain.

About two-thirds of the way up Cathedral Trail, I had to stop to rest and catch my breath. I was at the end of my rope and, with nowhere to go but up, I got a little teary. Our guide sat down beside me on a boulder to encourage me. He told me we were almost there, we were making good time, and it would be so worth it in the end. After a hug and a hand up, we completed the trail and within the hour reached the summit.

The view was breathtaking. We were able to spend some time at the top before heading back down a much easier but longer trail. We made it back to the bottom of the mountain just as it was turning dark.

When John and I were preparing for our wedding, I received a letter from our friend and guide. It read:

> *You must tell John, sometime, about that climb up Mt. Katahdin, and how you and your brothers chose Cathedral Trail, which is a steep and hard one, and how up there when the climbing was so hard you stopped and cried a little and thought you could not go on. And I put my arm around you and ... told you that you could go on because I would help you. And you did go on to the top and life will be this way for you, John and Mary. There will be times when you will sit down and cry and feel that you cannot go on. And then John will put his arms around you and tell you that you can go on because he will help you. And the two of you will go on together until the work is finished that God has called you to do.*

Adoption can feel overwhelming at times. The emotions, the questions, the unknowns for all involved can push us to our limits. Every issue that we experience can be turned into something that teaches and enables growth and maturity in us, if we allow it.

When I reflect on my life and all that God has brought me through and done for me along the way, I think of reaching the summit after a long climb. The view as we look back over our lives is breathtaking. Our faithful and covenant-keeping God has challenged us and helped us along the way to fulfill the course he has charted out for us. He has placed friends along the trail to encourage us and he has been with us every step of the way. Even when we were trying to climb on our own strength, it was he who directed our footsteps.

It reminds me that, when my life ends and I reach the summit of Heaven's gates, God will be there to welcome me. Not because of anything I have done, but because he loved me and sent his Son to die for me and rescue me from the death that I deserved.

Do you feel that hope too? It is the answer to traumatic loss and all of the issues seen in adoption. Without hope, our stories are bleak. We will be angry and overwhelmed. We will become victims of our circumstances and choices. But with even just a glimmer of hope, we will begin to see a way out of the darkness and into a light that shines brighter as we allow hope to grow within us.

I pray that all who seek hope will find Jesus. He is our ultimate hope and the writer of our stories.

I share the story Jesus has written for me so others can see his goodness. I share the hard times so generations to come can see his faithfulness. But mostly, I share this story so that others can be drawn closer to Jesus and experience that love and hope.

Are you sharing your story?

As children adopted by God, you and I have a story that people are desperate to hear. It's the gospel story. It's a story that gives hope. It's the story of redemption. I pray that it is your story too.

Questions for Thought

- What parts of your story do you struggle to see as part of God's good purpose?
- How do you see God using those hard parts of your story to form you into the person he is calling you to be?
- Do you have a spiritual adoption story? How can you share your story with others?

If you have questions about any of the Questions for Thought, please feel free to contact me for clarification. I would love to assist you in your search for truth or help you find someone who can answer these questions for you. My contact information is on the Author Page in the back of this book.

ACKNOWLEDGMENTS

I owe my deepest gratitude to many people for helping me imagine and believe in this book. From helping me develop the concept while relaxing on the back of a boat on the Chesapeake Bay to helping me dig deeper through conversations on a screened porch in West Virginia, friends who should be family pushed me to tell my story.

Thank you, Stephanie Hubach, for helping me to formulate my ideas into something readable and being one of my faithful cheerleaders throughout this project, just as you have been throughout my adult life. I like the way you think!

Thank you, Judy Aylestock, for being my first reader of the roughest early drafts and helping me proofread and edit it into something that could be read by a professional editor. Thank you, also, for the writing space and the cute "Writer in Residence" sign that provided encouragement to keep me going through the hard spots. You are a precious friend. Thank you for being there for me for over 40 years. You know too much!

Thank you, Lori Nyberg, for your generosity in allowing me to use your beach house as a writer's retreat. I will never forget finishing the final chapter and then walking along the beach praising God for how he has orchestrated my life. It will always be a sweet memory for me.

Thank you to the professional team that has helped me to execute a well-thought-out product. I am indebted to my editor, AnneMarie Spears, who made sense of my writings and shaped them into a beautiful product. Thank you to my writing group at Christian Book Academy and the many wonderful people there who have contributed thoughts, ideas, and prayers. Thank you to Katie Erickson for the book's cover art, for formatting, and for helping me navigate the details of publication.

Thank you to my manuscript readers:

Thank you, Kathy Azadian, for wading through the early rough draft and confirming things I needed clarity on. You were one of my first friends during a rough transition into life in Philadelphia in my teenage years—and the first person to ever suggest that I should write a book. You also told me that every girl needs a big brother, and now I have one! I cherish the friendship we have had for over 50 years.

Thank you to my "Adoption Readers": Amanda Brown, Rose B., Susan Ferrell, Gail Hall, and Denise Oorbeek. You each gave a unique perspective on the book through the lens of your adoption stories. Your vulnerability as you shared your story with me was a blessing I do not take for granted. I appreciate the time and effort you put into reading and reviewing the manuscript. I am blessed to know you and to have your perspective and encouragement.

My writing friends—Stephanie Buckwalter, Sage Costanza, and Stephanie Hubach—thank you for giving it to me straight. Your tough love improved my book. Your advice and suggestions were invaluable to the finished product. I treasure our friendship and I appreciated your professional side coming through, too.

My story could not be told without the love and support of my husband, John. Thank you, John, for letting me take large chunks of time away so I could stay focused on writing. You have been my rock and support through this project. Mostly, thank you for your part in my story. It hasn't always been easy, but it has always been good. God has been faithful despite our shortcomings. You are one of my life's biggest blessings.

I also thank God for the daily love and support of my children and grandchildren, for whom this book is written.

My greatest gratitude goes to my heavenly Father, who rescued me and redeemed me by the precious blood of his Son, Jesus. It is his adoption of me that redeems my story and secures my faith.

A WORD ABOUT DEPRESSION AND SUICIDAL IDEATION

If you are hurting, it is important that you seek help. **Text or call 988** if you are experiencing suicidal thoughts.

Depression is not just a feeling or emotion. It affects your body, your mind, and your spirit. Depression and the idea of suicide go hand in hand. When you are suffering from depression, you will ask yourself questions that lead to thinking about death. If you are thinking about dying, this is called suicidal ideation, also known as suicidal thoughts. These thoughts can come and go quickly, or they can move into contemplation and planning. If you have been experiencing suicidal thoughts, seek help. Tell someone what you are thinking.

There are many resources available today for all mental health struggles. You do not have to go through the pain and uncertainty alone. Your doctor, a counselor, or your pastor are all good places to start.

The causes of depression can be rooted in physical, mental, or spiritual health. Don't ignore any of these areas to find the root of the problem. Medication is not a crutch and can be useful short-term and long-term.

I benefited greatly from counseling from both my pastor and a professional therapist, along with medication. God used all three of these resources to help me lead a productive and joyful life.

Your greatest hope will be found in the Word of God. King David and Job are two examples of men who suffered from depression. David wrote many psalms where he cried out to God for relief. Psalms 6, 40, and 42 are good examples. He used phrases such as "my bones wasted away through my groaning all day long"[1] and "he brought me up from a desolate pit."[2] He wrote of his tears to describe the pain of depression: "I am weary from my groaning; with my tears I dampen my bed."[3]

There are also so many books and resources that I hesitate to recommend just one, but a recent addition to my list is *Depression: Finding Christ in the Darkness* by Edward T. Welch. Published in 2024, it is easy to read with short chapters. It can be used as a devotional or as a prompt for thinking or journaling.

Here are three hotlines if you or someone you know is struggling:

- **National Mental Health Hotline:** Call 866-903-3787 or go to mentalhealthhotline.org
- **National Suicide Prevention Hotline:** Call or text 988 or go to 988lifeline.org
- **Christians in Crisis Hotline:** Call or text 844-472-9687 or go to christiansncrisis.com

Why, my soul, are you downcast? Why so disturbed within me? Put your hope in God, for I will yet praise him, my Savior and my God.
—Psalm 42:5 NIV

END NOTES

Chapter 1: Growing A Family
1. Genesis 1:28 Christian Standard Bible
2. Genesis 17:7 CSB
3. John 3:16 CSB
4. 2 Timothy 3:15 CSB
5. George E. Haney Jr, "Northeast Outpost: Bangor, Maine," *The Orthodox* Presbyterian Messenger, April 1962,1.
6. 1 John 1:9 English Standard Version

Chapter 3: 'He's My Brother and I Have to Help Him'
1. John Bunyan, *The Pilgrim's Progress: In Modern English*, revised and updated by L. Edward Hazelbaker (Bridge-Logos, 1998), 153.
2. Bunyan, *The Pilgrim's Progress*, 154.
3. Bunyan, *The Pilgrim's Progress*, 204.

Chapter 4: 'I Am Not Blood'
1. Galatians 3:29 ESV
2. 2 Corinthians 5:17 ESV
3. Hebrews 12:1 New International Version

Chapter 5: Loss
1. Allison Davis Maxon and Sharon Kaplan Roszia, *The Seven Core Issues Workbook for Parents of Traumatized Children and Teens: A Guide to Help You Explore Feelings and Overcome Emotional*

Challenges in Your Family (Jessica Kingsley Publishers, 2022), 15.

2. Nancy Newton Verrier, *The Primal Wound: Understanding the Adopted Child* (Gateway Press,1993), 1.

3. Verrier, *The Primal Wound*, 20.

4. Robert A. Peterson, *Adopted by God: From Wayward Sinners to Cherished Children* (P&R Publishing, 2001), 87-88.

5. 1 John 4:19 CSB

6. Titus 2:14 CSB

7. Galatians 4:6 CSB

8. Psalm 139:16 CSB

9. Psalm 23:6 ESV

Chapter 6: Rejection

1. Sharon Kaplan Roszia and Allison Davis Maxon, *Seven Core Issues in Adoption and Permanency: A Comprehensive Guide to Promoting Understanding and Healing In Adoption, Foster Care, Kinship Families and Third Party Reproduction* (Jessica Kingsley Publishers, 2019), 62.

2. Roszia and Maxon, *Seven Core Issues*, 64.

3. Roszia and Maxon, *Seven Core Issues*, 65.

4. Marie Dolfi, "Core Issues of Adoption: An Adoption Trauma Paradigm," *Marie Dolfi*, June 1, 2024, https://mariedolfi.com/adoption-educational/core-issues-of-adoption-a-trauma-paradigm.

5. Roszia and Maxon, *Seven Core Issues*, 52.

6. Donna Kosick, ed., *The Gratitude Book Project: Celebrating 365 Days of Gratitude* (Donna Kosick Marketing, 2023).

7. Psalm 139:16 CSB

8. Jeremiah 29:11 CSB

9. Henry Harbaugh, trans., *The Heidelberg catechism, with proof-texts and explanations as used in the Palatinate* (D. Miller, 1892), "First Sabbath," question 1, https://www.loc.gov/item/22025629/.

Chapter 7: Shame and Guilt

1. Sharon Kaplan Roszia and Allison Davis Maxon, *Seven Core Issues in Adoption and Permanency: A Comprehensive Guide to Promoting Understanding and Healing In Adoption, Foster Care, Kinship Families and Third Party Reproduction* (Jessica Kingsley Publishers, 2019), 80.
2. C. John Miller, "Accepting God's Forgiveness: Believing in God's Love for You," in *CSB Life Counsel Bible* (Holman Bible Publishers, 2023), adapted from Miller, "Accepting God's Forgiveness: Believing in God's Love for You" (New Growth Press, 2011).
3. John 16:33 NIV
4. Matthew 11:28, 30 ESV
5. Miller, "Accepting God's Forgiveness."
6. Isaiah 30:18 CSB
7. Lamentations 3:22 NIV

Chapter 8: Grief

1. Sharon Kaplan Roszia and Allison Davis Maxon, *Seven Core Issues in Adoption and Permanency: A Comprehensive Guide to Promoting Understanding and Healing In Adoption, Foster Care, Kinship Families and Third Party Reproduction* (Jessica Kingsley Publishers, 2019),104.
2. Revelation 21:5 NIV
3. Bessel Van Der Kolk, *The Body Keeps the Score: Brain, Mind, and Body in the Healing of Trauma,* (Penguin Books, 2015).

4. Genesis 1:27 NIV
5. Lauren McAfee and Michael McAfee, *Beyond Our Control: Let Go of Unmet Expectations, Overcome Anxiety, and Discover Intimacy with God* (Thomas Nelson, 2023), 55.
6. Isaiah 43:2 ESV
7. Psalm 91:6 CSB
8. Patricia E. Clawson and Diane L. Olinger, ed., *Choosing the Good Portion: Women of the Orthodox Presbyterian Church* (The Committee for the Historian of the Orthodox Presbyterian Church, 2016), 213.
9. 1 Peter 5:7 CSB

Chapter 9: Identity

1. Allison Davis Maxon and Sharon Kaplan Roszia, *The Seven Core Issues Workbook for Parents of Traumatized Children and Teens: A Guide to Help You Explore Feelings and Overcome Emotional Challenges in Your Family* (Jessica Kingsley Publishers, 2022), 159.
2. Maxon and Roszia, *Seven Core Issues Workbook*, 159.
3. Maxon and Roszia, *Seven Core Issues Workbook*, 160.
4. Maxon and Roszia, *Seven Core Issues Workbook*, 160.
5. Romans 8:31 CSB
6. 2 Corinthians 4:17 CSB

Chapter 10: Intimacy

1. Allison Davis Maxon and Sharon Kaplan Roszia, *The Seven Core Issues Workbook for Parents of Traumatized Children and Teens: A Guide to Help*

You Explore Feelings and Overcome Emotional Challenges in Your Family (Jessica Kingsley Publishers, 2022), 183.

2. Patricia E. Clawson and Diane L. Olinger, ed., *Choosing the Good Portion: Women of the Orthodox Presbyterian Church* (The Committee for the Historian of the Orthodox Presbyterian Church, 2016), 215.

3. Lauren McAfee and Michael McAfee, *Beyond Our Control: Let Go of Unmet Expectations, Overcome Anxiety, and Discover Intimacy with God* (Thomas Nelson, 2023),

4. John 8:44 ESV

5. James 1:17 CSB

6. Romans 5:8 ESV

7. Psalm 139:17 ESV

Chapter 11: Mastery and Control

1. Allison Davis Maxon and Sharon Kaplan Roszia, *The Seven Core Issues Workbook for Parents of Traumatized Children and Teens: A Guide to Help You Explore Feelings and Overcome Emotional Challenges in Your Family* (Jessica Kingsley Publishers, 2022), 192.

2. Psalm 56:8 CSB

3. Lauren McAfee and Michael McAfee, *Beyond Our Control: Let Go of Unmet Expectations, Overcome Anxiety, and Discover Intimacy with God* (Thomas Nelson, 2023), 62.

4. Psalm 30:3 ESV

5. McAfee and McAfee, *Beyond Our Control*, 62.

6. Hebrews 13:5 CSB

7. Lamentations 3:22-23 CSB

8. McAfee and McAfee, Introduction to *Beyond Our Control.*
9. Jeremiah 29:11 CSB
10. Romans 6:17 ESV
11. Hebrews 11:1 ESV

Chapter 12: Telling Ourselves the Truth

1. John 8:32 ESV
2. Romans 5:12 CSB
3. John 3:16 ESV
4. John 14:6 ESV
5. John 1:12 ESV
6. Galatians 4:5 ESV
7. Zephaniah 3:17 ESV
8. Hebrews 13:5 CSB
9. 1 John 3:1 ESV
10. Ephesians 1:4 CSB
11. Isaiah 43:1 ESV
12. Isaiah 43:2 CSB
13. Psalm 91:1, 4 CSB
14. Romans 8:17 NIV
15. Galatians 4:7 ESV
16. Ephesians 2:19 CSB
17. Romans 8:26-27 ESV
18. Hebrews 12:1 CSB
19. Paul David Tripp, *Helping Your Adopted Child: Understanding Your Child's Unique Identity* (New Growth Press, 2008), 7.

Chapter 13: The Truth About Adoption

1. Psalm 139:16 CSB
2. Isaiah 43:18-19 CSB
3. Revelation 21:5 CSB
4. 2 Corinthians 5:17 CSB

5. Revelation 21:1 CSB

6. John 14:3 CSB

7. Jeremiah 29:11 CSB

8. Marie Dolfi, "Core Issues of Adoption: An Adoption Trauma Paradigm," *Marie Dolfi*, June 1, 2024, https://mariedolfi.com/adoption-educational/core-issues-of-adoption-a-trauma-paradigm.

9. Dolfi, "Core Issues of Adoption."

10. Back cover review to *Adoption Unfiltered: Revelations from Adoptees, Birth Parents, Adoptive Parents, and Allies,* by Sara Easterly, Kelsey Vander Vliet Ranyard, and Lori Holden (Rowman & Littlefield Publishers, 2024).

11. B.K. Jackson, back cover review to *Adoption Unfiltered,* by Easterly et al.

12. Easterly et al, *Adoption Unfiltered,* 118.

13. Easterly et al, *Adoption Unfiltered,* 119.

14. Easterly et al, *Adoption Unfiltered,* 119.

15. Russell D. Moore, *Adopted for Life: The Priority of Adoption for Christian Families and Churches* (Crossway, 2009), 190.

16. John 16:33 NIV

17. Romans 8:15 NIV

18. Ephesians 6:17 ESV

19. Ruth Chou Simons, *Now and Not Yet: Pressing in When You're Waiting, Wanting, and Restless for More* (Thomas Nelson, 2024), 147.

20. Romans 12:2 NIV

21. 2 Corinthians 10:5 NIV

22. Isaiah 43:1 CSB

23. John 9:1-3 CSB

24. Psalm 31:3 ESV

Chapter 14: Finding Hope in the Truth

1. Ralph Waldo Emerson, "The complete works of Ralph Waldo Emerson: Letters and social aims [Vol. 8]," in *The Complete Works of Ralph Waldo Emerson* (University of Michigan Library Digital Collections), 338, June 5, 2025, https://name.umdl.umich.edu/4957107.0008.001.
2. Isaiah 45:3 CSB
3. Isaiah 41:10 NIV
4. Psalm 139:16 CSB
5. Luke 12:7 CSB
6. 1 Peter 5:7 CSB
7. Isaiah 46:4 NIV

BIBLIOGRAPHY

Bunyan, John. *The Pilgrim's Progress: In Modern English.* Revised and updated by L. Edward Hazelbaker. Bridge-Logos, 1998.

Clawson, Patricia E. and Diane L. Olinger, ed. *Choosing the Good Portion*: *Women of the Orthodox Presbyterian Church.* The Committee for the Historian of the Orthodox Presbyterian Church, 2016.

Dolfi, Marie. "Core Issues of Adoption: An Adoption Trauma Paradigm." *Marie Dolfi.* https://mariedolfi.com/adoption-educational/core-issues-of-adoption-a-trauma-paradigm.

Easterly, Sara, Kelsey Vander Vliet Ranyard and Lori Holden. *Adoption Unfiltered: Revelations from Adoptees, Birth Parents, Adoptive Parents, and Allies.* Rowman & Littlefield Publishers, 2024.

Emerson, Ralph Waldo. "The complete works of Ralph Waldo Emerson: Letters and social aims [Vol. 8]." In *The Complete Works of Ralph Waldo Emerson.* University of Michigan Library Digital Collections. https://name.umdl.umich.edu/4957107.0008.001.

Harbaugh, Henry, trans. *The Heidelberg catechism, with proof-texts and explanations as used in the Palatinate.* D Miller, 1892. https://www.loc.gov/item/22025629.

Kosick, Donna, ed. *The Gratitude Book Project: Celebrating 365 Days of Gratitude.* Donna Kosick Marketing, 2023.

Maxon, Allison Davis and Sharon Kaplan Roszia. *The Seven Core Issues Workbook for Parents of Traumatized Children and Teens: A Guide to Help You Explore*

Feelings and Overcome Emotional Challenges in Your Family. Jessica Kingsley Publishers, 2022.

McAfee, Lauren and Michael McAfee. *Beyond Our Control: Let Go of Unmet Expectations, Overcome Anxiety, and Discover Intimacy with God.* Nelson Books, 2023.

Miller, C. John. "Accepting God's Forgiveness: Believing in God's Love for You." In *CSB Life Counsel* Bible. Holman Bible Publishers, 2023. Adapted from Miller, "Accepting God's Forgiveness: Believing in God's Love for You." New Growth Press, 2011.

Moore, Russell D. *Adopted for Life: The Priority of Adoption for Christian Families and Churches.* Crossway Books, 2009.

Packer, J.I. *Knowing God.* InterVarsity Press, 1973.

Peterson, Robert A. *Adopted by God: From Wayward Sinners to Cherished Children.* P&R Publishing, 2001.

Roszia, Sharon Kaplan and Allison Davis Maxon. *A Comprehensive Guide to Promoting Understanding and Healing In Adoption, Foster Care, Kinship Families and Third Party Reproduction.* Jessica Kingsley Publishers, 2019.

Simons, Ruth Chou. *Now and Not Yet: Pressing in When You're Waiting, Wanting, and Restless for More.* Thomas Nelson, 2024.

Soehnlin, Jenn. *On the Same Page with God: Embracing the Power of Praying Scripture.* Autograph Publishing, 2024.

Tripp, Paul David. *Helping Your Adopted Child: Understanding Your Child's Unique Identity.* New Growth Press, 2008.

Verrier, Nancy Newton. *The Primal Wound: Understanding the Adopted Child.* Gateway Press, 1993.

ABOUT THE AUTHOR

Mary Haney Underwood understands personally the challenges found in the complexities of adoption. In *Adopted Twice,* she shares her story of adoption with candor and grace. She combines personal stories with biblical wisdom, inviting readers to embrace their stories as part of God's greater narrative. *Adopted Twice* points readers to Christ's transformative power for answers to their deepest longings and often unspoken struggles.

Mary cherishes her roles as a daughter of the King, wife, mother, and "Grandmary." While *Adopted Twice* is her first book, her writing has been featured in devotionals, blogs and social media platforms. Mary also finds joy in gardening, crafting, and reading. She lives in Virginia with her husband, John.

Mary has been previously published in:

- *A Year of Favor: 365 Inspirational Devotionals Celebrating God's Unstoppable Goodness,* edited by Benecia Ponder. Her essay "Do I Trust Him?" can be found in "Week 19: The Favor of Trust."
- *The Gratitude Book Project: Celebrating 365 Days of Gratitude,* 2024 edition, edited by Donna Kozik. Her essay "Grateful She Chose Life" can be found on April 14. Her award-winning essay "True Freedom" can be found on July 4.

Contact information for Mary Haney Underwood
mary@maryhaneyunderwood.com
www.whatemptynest.com

www.ingramcontent.com/pod-product-compliance
Lightning Source LLC
Chambersburg PA
CBHW071219090426
42736CB00014B/2901